Janice VanCleave's

BIG BOOK OF
PLAY AND
FIND OUT
Science Projects

JB JOSSEY-BASS

Janice VanCleave's

BIG BOOK OF
PLAY AND
FIND OUT
Science Projects

Janice VanCleave

BICENTENNIAL
1807
WILEY
2007
BICENTENNIAL

John Wiley & Sons, Inc.

Published by Jossey-Bass
A Wiley Imprint
989 Market Street, San Francisco, CA 94103-1741
www.josseybass.com

Design and composition by Navta Associates, Inc.

Wiley Bicentennial Logo: Richard J. Pacifico

Portions of this book have been previously published in the books *Janice VanCleave's Play and Find Out about Science*, © 1996 Janice VanCleave; *Janice VanCleave's Play and Find Out about Nature*, © 1997 Janice VanCleave; *Janice VanCleave's Play and Find Out about the Human Body*, © 1998 Janice VanCleave; *Janice VanCleave's Play and Find Out about Bugs*, © 1999 Janice VanCleave.

The publisher and the author have made every reasonable effort to insure that the experiments and activities in the book are safe when conducted as instructed but assume no responsibility for any damage caused or sustained while performing the experiments or activities in this book. Parents, guardians, and/or teachers should supervise young readers who undertake the experiments and activities in this book.

Jossey-Bass books and products are available through most bookstores. To contact Jossey-Bass directly, call our Customer Care Department within the United States at 800-956-7739, outside the United States at 317-572-3986, or fax 317-572-4002.

Jossey-Bass also publishes its books in a variety of electronic formats. Some content that appears in print may not be available in electronic books.

Library of Congress Cataloging-in-Publication Data

VanCleave, Janice Pratt.
 [Big book of play and find out science projects]
 Janice VanCleave's big book of play and find out science projects / Janice VanCleave.
   p. cm.
 Includes bibliographical references and index.
 ISBN 978-0-7879-8928-6 (pbk.)
 1. Science projects—Juvenile literature. 2. Science—Experiments—Juvenile literature.
 3. Science—Study and teaching (Primary)—Juvenile literature. I. Title.
 Q164.V384 2006
 507.8—dc22

                                                         2006052572

Printed in the United States of America
first edition

10 9 8 7 6 5 4 3 2 1

Contents

Part Three   BUGS   99

Part Four   THE HUMAN BODY   149

A Letter from
Janice VanCleave

Dear Friends,

Welcome to science playtime!

The scientific play activities in this book are about chemistry, physics, and biology. Very young children may not know the words "chemistry" or "physics" or "biology," but give them a recipe for bouncy blubber or a magnet, or send them out on a bug-collecting expedition, and watch their eyes light up!

Discovering things on their own gives kids a wonderful feeling of success. All they need is your friendly guidance, a few good ideas, and their natural curiosity. This book is full of fun ideas. It contains instructions for more than 50 simple, hands-on experiments inspired by questions from real kids. While you play together, your child will find out the answers to questions such as "Why do balls bounce?" "Why do dogs pant?" and lots of other things that children wonder about.

So get ready to enter into a science adventure.

Playfully yours,

Janice VanCleave

Before You Begin

1 **Read the experiment completely before starting.** When possible, practice the experiment by yourself prior to your science playtime. This increases your understanding of the topic and makes you more familiar with the procedure and the materials. If you know the experiment well, it will be easier for you to give your child instructions and answer questions. For more information about the basic science behind each experiment, see Appendix A.

2 **Select a place to work.** The kitchen table is usually the best place for the experiments. It provides space and access to an often needed water supply.

3 **Choose a time.** There is no best time to play with your child, and play should be the main point when doing the experiments in this book. Select a time when you will have the fewest distractions so that you can complete the experiment. If your family has a schedule, you may allot a specific amount of time for the experiment. You may want to set an exact starting time so that the child can watch the clock and become more familiar with time. Try to schedule 5 to 10 minutes at the close of each session to have everyone clean up.

4 **Collect supplies.** You will have less frustration and more fun if all the materials are ready before you start. (See "Tips on Materials" in the box on the next page.)

5 **Do not rush through the experiment.** Follow each step carefully, and for sure and safe results, never skip steps or add your own. Safety is of the utmost importance, and it is a good technique to teach children to follow instructions when doing an experiment.

6 **Have fun!** Don't worry if the child isn't "getting" the science principle, or if the results aren't exactly perfect. If you feel the results are too different from those described, reread the instructions and start over from step 1.

7 **Enjoy the wonder of participating in the learning process.** Remember, it is OK for your child not to discover the scientific explanation. For example,

when you perform the experiment "Springy," the child may be too excited about testing his flea hopper to stop and listen to your explanation of why fleas jump so high. Don't force the child to listen. Join in the fun and make a magic moment to remember. Later, when questions about jumping bugs arise, you can remind the child of the fun time that you had doing the "Springy" experiment and then repeat the experiment, providing the explanation.

Tips on Materials

- Some experiments call for water. If you want everything to be at the worktable, you can supply water in a pitcher or soda bottle.

- Extra paper towels are always handy for accidental spills, especially if the experiment calls for liquids. A large bowl can be used for waste liquids, and the bowl can be emptied in the sink later.

- To save time, you can precut some of the materials (except string; see below).

- Do not cut string in advance, because it generally gets tangled and is difficult to separate. You and the child can measure and cut the string together.

- You may want to keep labeled shoe boxes filled with basic materials that are used in many experiments, such as scissors, tape, marking pens, and so forth.

- The specific sizes and types of paper or other listed materials are those used when these experiments were tested. This doesn't mean that substituting a different type of material will result in a failed experiment. Substitution of materials should be a value judgment made after you have read an experiment to determine the use of the material. For example, you could replace an index card with a stiff piece of paper of comparable suggested size.

- For large groups, multiply the material by the number in the group so that each person can perform the experiment individually. Some of the materials (like glue) can be shared, so read the procedure ahead of time to determine quantities.

Part One | # PHYSICAL SCIENCE

Air

Spacey

round up these things

bowl, at least 4 inches (10 cm) tall and
   6 inches (15 cm) in diameter
ruler
tap water
paper towel
3-ounce (90-ml) paper cup

later you'll need

1-gallon (1-liter) resealable plastic bag
CAUTION: *Never let young children play
with plastic bags on their own. Put the
bag safely away after the experiment.*

1 Fill the bowl with about 3 inches (7.5 cm) of water.

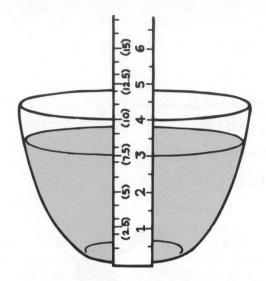

2 Crumple the paper towel into a ball and push it into the inside bottom of the cup.

3 Turn the cup upside down. The crumpled towel must remain against the bottom of the cup. If the towel moves or falls out, uncrumple it a little.

4 Hold the cup upside down. Push the cup straight down into the bowl of water until the mouth of the cup touches the bottom of the bowl. NOTE: *Do not tilt the cup.*

5 Lift the cup out of the water, again without tilting the cup.

6 Remove the crumpled towel from the cup and examine it. The towel will still be dry.

So Now We Know

Air is easy to catch, because it's all around you. Air fills all the empty spaces in a room. Air also fills an empty paper cup. When you put the cup in the bowl of water, the air in the cup kept the water away from the paper towel.

Catch some air in the resealable plastic bag by opening the bag and moving it through the air. Seal the bag, then squeeze it between your hands. You cannot see the air inside the bag, but you know it is there because the bag is inflated and it changes shape as you push the air around inside the bag.

Drifter

I wonder...
What holds up
a parachute?

Let's find
out!

round up these things

scissors
ruler
string
transparent tape
sheet of typing paper
2 small paper clips
grape-size piece of modeling clay

later you'll need

parachute and clay figure from original
 experiment
          plus
grape-size piece of modeling clay
small paper clip

1 Cut four 12-inch (30-cm) pieces of string.

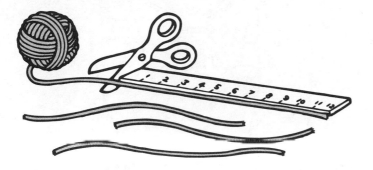

2 Tape one end of each piece of string to each of the four corners of the sheet of paper.

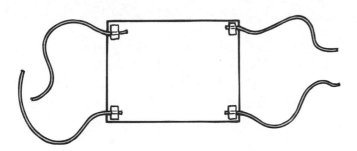

3 Lay the paper on a table with the tape side down. Bring the four free ends of the strings together and wrap a piece of tape around them.

4 Open a paper clip to make a hook. Tape the paper clip to the tape on the ends of the strings. You have made a parachute.

5 Shape a figure out of the clay and press it onto the other paper clip so that a small part of one end of the paper clip extends above the figure.

6 Attach the clip of the clay figure to the hook on the parachute.

7 Hold the short ends of the paper part of the parachute so that the clay figure hangs down.

8 Raise the parachute in your hands as high as possible.

9 Drop the parachute. It and the clay figure will slowly fall.

So Now We Know

Air fills and pushes up on the inside of a falling parachute. This makes the parachute fall slowly. Your clay figure floated down gently because it was attached to a parachute.

More Fun Things to Know and Do

Make a second clay figure the same size as the first one and press it onto a paper clip. The two figures should weigh about the same. Hold your paper parachute as before with its clay figure attached to the hook. At the same time, ask your helper to hold the second clay figure so that the two figures are at the same height. On the count of three, drop both clay figures and watch to determine which one hits the ground first.

Changes

Bouncy Blubber

round up these things

1 quart (1 liter) distilled water
1 tablespoon (15 ml) borax (a water
  softener sold as a laundry aid)
1-quart (1-liter) jar
spoon
timer
coffee cup
4-ounce (120-ml) bottle of white school
  glue
bowl
cold tap water
resealable plastic bag
paper towel
marking pen
CAUTION: *Keep the box of borax away
  from small children and do not allow
  them to drink the borax solution. See
  the warning on the box.*

later you'll need

bouncy blubber from original experiment

1 Put the distilled water and the borax in the jar. Stir.

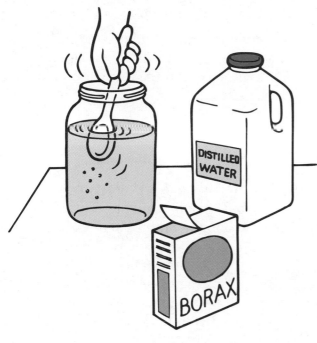

2 Wait 5 minutes to allow any undissolved borax to settle to the bottom of the jar.

3 Fill the cup three-fourths full with the borax solution.

4 **Adult Step** Hold the glue bottle upside down above the cup of borax, then squeeze the bottle so that a steady, thin stream of glue falls into the cup.

5 Use the spoon to keep stirring as the glue enters the cup.

6 A white stringlike mass will form and wrap around the spoon.

7 **Adult Step** When the spoon becomes coated, stop squeezing the glue bottle.

8 With your hands, pull the white mass, which we'll call bouncy blubber, off the spoon and put it in a bowl of cold water.

9 Remove the bouncy blubber and lay it on top of the plastic bag.

10 Dry your hands with the paper towel.

11 Squeeze the bouncy blubber in your hands for about 20 to 30 seconds.

12 Shape the bouncy blubber into a ball by gently pressing and rolling it between your hands.

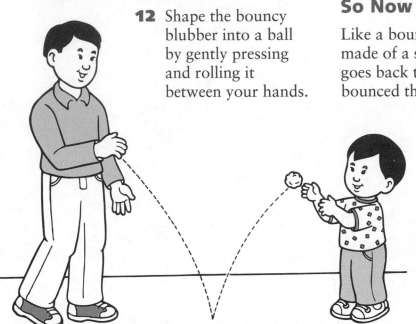

13 Bounce your bouncy blubber ball on a table or on a tile floor.

14 Repeat steps 3 through 11 to make more bouncy blubber.

15 Store your bouncy blubber in the resealable bag. Label the bag Do Not Eat and place it in the refrigerator to prevent mold.

So Now We Know

Like a bouncy blubber ball, most balls are made of a stretchy material that always goes back to its original shape. When you bounced the bouncy blubber ball on the floor, the side of the ball that hit the floor was pushed in. But because the ball is made of stretchy material, the pushed-in side went back to its original shape and pushed against the floor, making the ball bounce.

More Fun Things to Know and Do

Balls that are to be bounced are usually round because you can control the direction that a round ball bounces. If you throw a round ball straight down, it bounces straight up. But you cannot control the direction of the bounce of a ball that is not round. Shape the bouncy blubber into other shapes, such as a cube or a pyramid. Compare the bounciness of the different shapes.

I wonder how a square ball would bounce.

Play Clay

1 cup (250 ml) flour
½ cup (125 ml) table salt
2 tablespoons (30 ml) cream of tartar
2-quart (2-liter) bowl
spoon
¾ cup (188 ml) tap water
saucepan
oven mitt
1 tablespoon (15 ml) cooking oil
timer
1-quart (1-liter) resealable plastic bag

later you'll need

the same materials
          plus
food coloring
NOTE: *Even though the play clay is nontoxic, it should not be eaten because it contains a large amount of salt.*

1 Put the flour, salt, and cream of tartar in the bowl.

2 Mix thoroughly with the spoon.

3 Pour the water into the saucepan.

4 Adult Step Heat the water to boiling.

5 Adult Step Use the oven mitt to remove the pan from the stove.

6 Adult Step Add the oil to the hot water.

7 Adult Step Slowly pour the hot liquid into the bowl that contains the flour mixture, stirring as the liquid is being added.

8 Wait 5 minutes or until the mixture is cool enough to handle. Then, thoroughly mix the play clay by squeezing it between your hands.

9 Mold the play clay into different shapes, such as people, dinosaurs, or flowers.

10 Store the clay in the resealable bag.

So Now We Know

When you mix things together and heat them, they often turn into something else. Flour, salt, water, and oil in certain amounts make play clay (which you shouldn't eat because of the high amount of salt), but flour, sugar, milk, and oil in other amounts make cookies!

More Fun Things to Know and Do

The clay can be colored by adding food coloring to the hot liquid before adding the liquid to the flour mixture. Repeat the experiment, using about 20 drops of food coloring.

Magnets

FOLD LINE

Stickers

round up these things

refrigerator magnet (a disk magnet used in
  the experiment "North Seekers" will
  work)
sheet of paper
pencil
ruler
scissors
rubber band
3 to 4 small metal paper clips

later you'll need

pencil
sheet of typing paper
ruler
scissors
crayons
transparent tape
3 to 5 small metal paper clips
shoe box
magnet

1 Lay the magnet on the paper.

2 Draw a rectangle on the paper that is about the same width as the magnet and about 2 inches (5 cm) longer.

|←2 in.→|
(5 cm)

3 Cut out the rectangle from the paper.

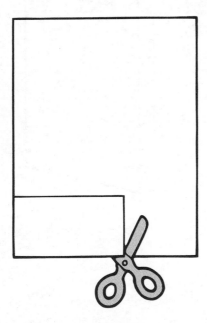

4 Hold the magnet close to, but not touching, the paper rectangle. Observe whether the paper moves toward the magnet. The paper does not move, which means that the paper is not attracted to the magnet.

5 Wrap the paper rectangle around the magnet and secure it with the rubber band.

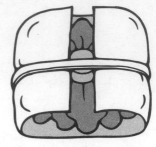

6 Place the paper clips on a nonmetal table.

7 Hold the paper-wrapped magnet about 6 inches (15 cm) above the paper clips.

8 Slowly lower the magnet. The paper clips will move toward the magnet. This means that the power of the magnet moves through the paper and attracts the metal paper clips.

So Now We Know

Magnets have a force that pulls them toward metal things, such as paper clips and refrigerators. This force works even through paper! That's why your drawings stay stuck to the refrigerator.

When a magnet moves, its magnetic force moves with it. A paper clip attracted to a magnet through a sheet of paper will move where the magnet moves. You can use a magnet this way to put on a puppet show.

- Draw and cut out 3 to 5 paper figures, similar to the one shown here. Use crayons to draw faces and clothes on the figures.

- Tape a paper clip to the base of each figure. Remember that you want the figure to be as light as possible, so don't use too much tape.

- Fold the base under along the fold line.

- Use an open shoe box for a stage. Stand the shoe box so that its open end faces you.

- Place the paper figures on top of the box. Hold the magnet inside the box under one of the figures. Move the figure by moving the magnet.

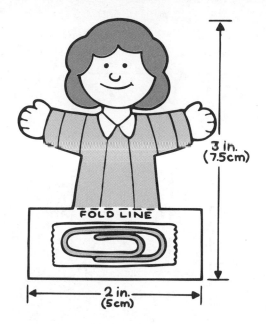

3 in. (7.5cm)

FOLD LINE

2 in. (5cm)

North Seekers

round up these things

masking tape
sheet of paper
compass
marking pen
6-inch (15-cm) piece of string
2 disk magnets of equal size

later you'll need

disk magnet from original experiment
         plus
small paper clip
8-inch (20-cm) piece of thread
timer
pencil
tall, clear drinking glass
NOTE: *Never touch a compass with a magnet. Touching a compass with a strong magnet can change the polarity of the compass needle, causing the pole marked north to become a south pole and all directions to be reversed.*

1 Tape the sheet of paper to the top of a nonmetal table. Be sure that there are no magnetic materials on or near the table.

2 Place the compass in the center of the paper and watch the compass needle move. Slowly rotate the compass until the colored part of the compass needle points to the N on the compass.

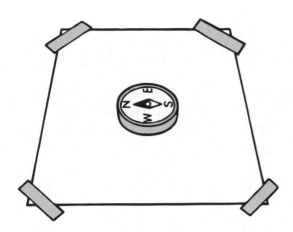

3 Use the marking pen to make a mark on the paper at the north and south compass points.

4 Remove the compass.

5 Label the directions N and S with the pen. Draw an arrow connecting the two points. You have made a paper compass.

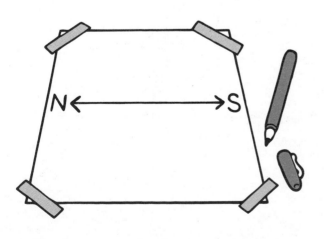

6 Tape the string to the rounded edge of one of the disk magnets. Keep the other magnet away from the table.

7 Holding the free end of the string, hang the magnet over the paper compass until the magnet's flat sides point steadily in a north-to-south direction.

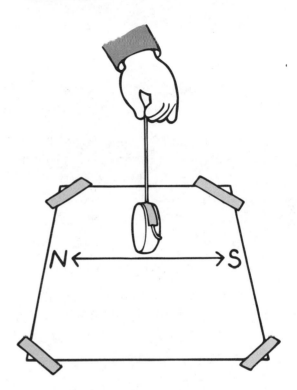

8 Use the tape and the marking pen to label the side of the magnet that points north with a large dot and the side that points south with a large X.

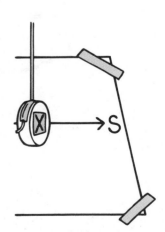

9 Remove the string from the magnet.

10 Repeat steps 6 through 9 to label the flat sides of the second magnet. Keep these magnets for the experiment "Pushers."

So Now We Know

The needle inside a compass is a little magnet that can swing around. One end of the needle always points north. The hanging disk magnet also swung around so that one side pointed north. Every magnet has a north end and a south end. The dots mark the north end of each magnet, and the X marks their south end.

More Fun Things to Know and Do

A paper clip can be magnetized by laying it on top of a magnet. This magnetized paper clip will point north if it is hung from a thread.

To see this happen:

- Clip the paper clip to one end of the 8-inch (20-cm) piece of thread.

- Lay the narrow end of the paper clip across the X on the magnet.

- After about 2 minutes, remove the paper clip from the magnet and tie the free end of the thread to the center of the pencil. The narrow end of the magnetized paper clip is the north end.

- Lay the pencil across the mouth of the glass so that the paper clip is suspended in the glass and is protected from air currents. Watch what happens to the paper clip.

Forces

Floater

round up these things

2-quart (2-liter) bowl
cold tap water
2 walnut-size pieces of modeling clay

later you'll need

two 1-quart (1-liter) jars
cold tap water
6 to 9 tablespoons (90 to 135 ml) table
  salt
2 small uncooked eggs of equal size
spoon

1 Fill the bowl three-fourths full with cold tap water.

2 Shape one piece of clay into a ball by rolling it around between the palms of your hands.

3 Carefully place the clay ball on the surface of the water in the bowl. The ball will sink.

4 Remove the clay ball from the water and set it aside.

5 Shape the second piece of clay so that it looks like a boat. Make the bottom of the boat as large as possible and the sides short. NOTE: *Young children may need some assistance in shaping the boat.*

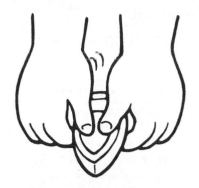

6 Gently place the clay boat on the surface of the water in the bowl. The boat will float.

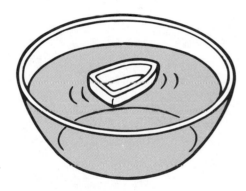

So Now We Know

Boats float because of their shape. The weight of the boat is spread out over more water, so there is more water underneath the boat to hold it up.

Boats float better in the saltwater of oceans than in the freshwater of rivers and lakes, because saltwater weighs more and pushes up on objects more.

- Fill each jar half full with water.

- Stir 6 tablespoons (90 ml) of salt into one of the jars of water.

- Set one of the eggs on the spoon, tilt one of the jars, and gently lower the egg into the jar.

- Place the other egg in the second jar. Observe how high each egg floats.

NOTE: *Since the weight of eggs varies, you might need to add more salt to make the egg in the saltwater float near the surface.*

Buckle Up

round up these things

4-by-12-inch (10-by-30-cm) piece of stiff
  cardboard (size is not critical)
book, about 1 inch (2.5 cm) thick
masking tape
pencil
walnut-size piece of modeling clay
small toy car
12-inch (30-cm) piece of ¼-inch (0.6-cm)
  ribbon (or any narrow ribbon)

later you'll need

the same materials
    plus
another book about 1 inch (2.5 cm) thick

1 Place one end of the cardboard on the edge of the book.

2 Tape the other end of the cardboard to a table.

3 Tape the pencil to the table about two toy-car lengths from the taped end of the cardboard.

6 Position the car and clay figure at the raised end of the cardboard.

7 Release the car and watch it roll down the cardboard and collide into the pencil. The car will stop, but the clay figure will sail through the air.

4 Make a clay figure shaped like a snowman.

5 Flatten the bottom of the clay figure and gently rest it on the hood of the toy car. Do not press the clay onto the car.

8 Use the ribbon to tie the clay figure to the car, and then repeat steps 6 and 7. The clay figure will stay on the car.

So Now We Know

Moving objects continue to move forward until something stops them. The seat belt, like the ribbon around the clay figure, keeps you from getting hurt when a car suddenly stops. If you are wearing a seat belt, then the seat belt stops you. If you are not wearing a seat belt, then you keep going until something like the dashboard or the front seat stops you.

When riding in a car, you, like the clay figure, are moving at the same speed as the car. The toy car will reach a faster speed if the cardboard is raised higher. If the clay figure is not secured to the car with ribbon, the figure will fly farther through the air.

Raise the cardboard by placing the second book on top of the first one. Repeat the experiment, noticing how far away from the pencil the figure lands.

Light

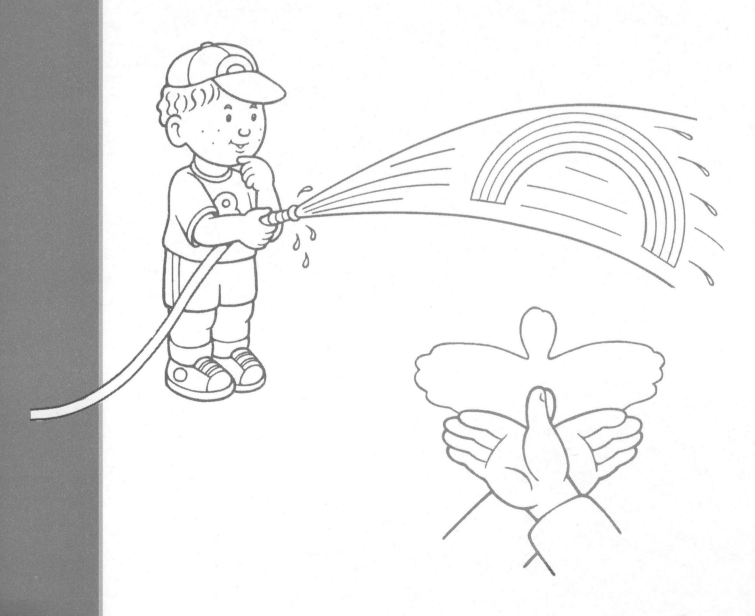

Changing

round up these things	later you'll need
index card	spring tension rod that extends 28 to 48 inches (70 to 120 cm)
walnut-size piece of modeling clay	white sheet
pencil with eraser	4 large safety pins
flashlight	desk lamp or lamp without a shade
ruler	yardstick (meterstick)

1 Lay the index card on a table.

2 Place the piece of modeling clay on the card.

3 Stand the pencil upright, eraser end up, in the clay.

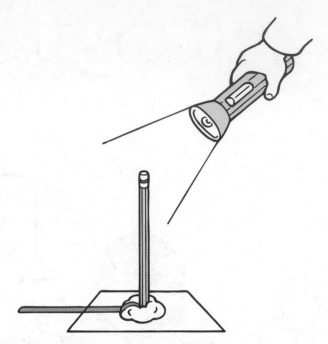

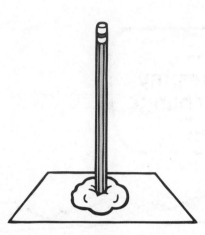

4 Turn the flashlight on.

5 Darken the room.

6 Hold the flashlight so that it is to one side of the pencil and about 4 inches (10 cm) from the eraser. Notice the length of the shadow.

8 Hold the flashlight so that it is directly above the eraser and the same distance away as in step 6. Little or no shadow will be produced.

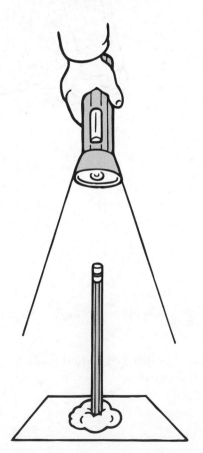

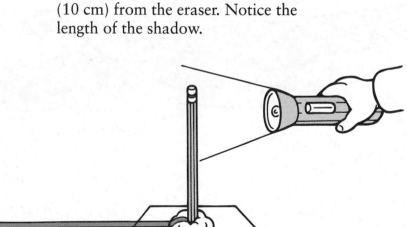

7 Hold the flashlight so that it is at an angle to the eraser and the same distance away as in step 6. The shadow will be shorter.

So Now We Know

Shadows change size as the position of the light that makes them changes. Your shadow appears when your body gets between the sun and the ground.

When the sun, like the flashlight, is high overhead, the shadow is short. When the sun is low in the sky, the shadow is long.

More Fun Things to Know and Do

1 Light travels in a straight line and cannot bend around materials, so shadows have the same shape as the object that blocks the light. You can put on an animal-shadow show by positioning your hands and fingers so that they block light and create shadows in the shape of animals.

- Place the spring tension rod across an open doorway.

- Hang the white sheet by lapping it over the rod and securing with the safety pins. This will be your screen.

- Place the lamp about 2 yards (2 m) from the screen.

- Turn on the lamp, then darken the room.

- Hold your hands between the lamp and the screen so that your hands are about 6 inches (15 cm) from the screen.

- Position your fingers to make the animal shadows shown. Experiment to make other animal shadows.

2 The closer an object is to the light, the more light the object blocks. You can change the size of your animal shadows by changing your distance from the lamp. To produce a larger

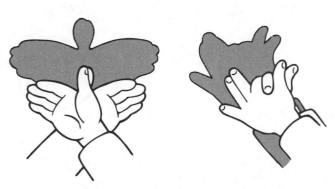

shadow on the screen, hold your hands closer to the lamp. To make a smaller shadow, stand farther from the lamp. CAUTION: *Do not hold your hands closer than 6 inches (15 cm) from the lamp. The heat from the bulb could burn your skin.*

Rainbows

garden hose
spray nozzle (optional)

1-quart (1-liter) glass jar
tap water
sheet of typing paper

1. Turn the water on and adjust the nozzle on the hose so that it sprays a fine mist of water. *NOTE: If you don't have a spray nozzle, you can get the same effect by holding your thumb partially over the opening of the hose.*

2. Standing with the sun behind you, hold the hose so that the water sprays into the air in front of you. Move the spray from side to side until you see a rainbow in the mist. CAUTION: *Never look directly at the sun, because doing so can permanently damage your eyes.*

So Now We Know

Rainbows happen when sunlight passes through water drops. The light is separated into the seven rainbow colors: red, orange, yellow, green, blue, indigo, and violet.

More Fun Things to Know and Do

Light passing through a glass container of water will separate into rainbow colors.

- Fill the jar with water.

- Place the jar indoors on a window ledge or table edge near a window. The sun must be shining directly in the window.

- Place the sheet of white paper on the shadow of the jar on the floor. Watch the rainbow appear on the paper.

Sound

String Telephone

round up these things

pencil
9-ounce (270-ml) paper cup
9-foot (2.7-m) string
paper clip

later you'll need

pencil
four 9-ounce (270-ml) paper cups
two 9-yard (8-m) strings
4 paper clips
3 helpers

1 **Adult Step** Use the pencil to make a small hole in the bottom of the cup.

2 Thread the end of the string through the hole and into the cup.

3 Knot the end of the string. To keep the knot from pulling through the hole, attach the paper clip to the string between the knot and the cup.

4 Tie the free end of the string to a doorknob.

5 Walk away from the door until the string is taut.

6 Hold the cup to your ear while a helper gently strums, rubs, then blows on the string near the doorknob. You will hear the sounds loud and clear in the cup.

7 Trade places with your helper and repeat steps 5 and 6.

So Now We Know

In telephones that have wires, the sound travels through the wire from one telephone to another. In your string telephone, the sound traveled through a string from one place to another.

1 Telephones send the sound of voices. A two-cup string telephone can also send voice sounds. Make another telephone, using two cups and one of the longer strings.

- Attach a cup to each end of the string. Take the string telephone outside.

- Ask your helper to hold one cup while you hold the other.

- Walk away from your helper until the string is taut between you.

- Take turns with your helper as one person speaks into one cup and the other listens through the other cup.

2 The sound in the string will be sent to anything the string touches. If the strings of two string telephones cross each other, three people will hear the voice of the person speaking.

- Make another two-cup telephone as in the previous experiment.

- Have two helpers (A and B) hold the cups of one telephone and walk away from each other until the string is taut between them.

- Ask a third helper (C) to help you (D) wrap the middle of the string of the other telephone once around the middle of the first telephone's string.

- Walk away from each other until the string of the second telephone is taut. Take turns speaking into the cups.

Musical Teeth

round up these things

craft stick

later you'll need

1-yard (1-m) string
wire clothes hanger
metal spoon

1 Place one end of the craft stick between your teeth.

2 Gently rub your finger against the other end of the stick. You will hear a loud rubbing sound.

3 Hold the stick in one hand, and with the finger of your other hand, gently rub the other end of the stick. You will hear a low rubbing sound or no sound at all.

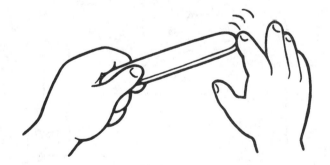

So Now We Know

Sounds that travel through air aren't as loud as sounds that travel through solids. Most of the noise you make when you chew is heard only by you. This is because the sound goes through the bones in your head right to your ears, not into the air.

1 Bells and chimes are made of metal because metals make sounds easily. A wire clothes hanger makes a sound like chimes.

- Wrap one end of the string around one finger of each hand.

- Hang the clothes hanger on the string so that it hangs freely.

- Ask your helper to tap the hanger several times with the spoon.

2 The sound of your clothes hanger chimes can be made louder if the sounds travel to your ear through a solid.

- With the strings wrapped around your two fingers as before, place your fingertips just inside your ears, being careful not to poke into your ears.

- Lean forward slightly so that the hanger does not touch your body.

- Ask your helper to tap the hanger several times with the spoon.

Electricity

Attractive

I wonder . . . Why does my hair stick to my comb?

Let's find out!

round up these things

9-inch (23-cm) round balloon

later you'll need

balloon from original experiment
    plus
paper hole-punch
sheet of tissue paper or other thin paper
12-inch (30-cm) long balloon
NOTE: *These experiments work best when the humidity is very low.*

1 Inflate the balloon to a size that fits easily in your hand.

2 Adult Step Tie a knot in the end of the balloon.

3 Rub the inflated balloon back and forth on your hair about 10 times. NOTE: *For best results your hair must be clean, dry, and oil-free.*

4 Slowly pull the balloon away from your hair and hold it close to, but not touching, your head. Your hair will lift and stick to the balloon.

So Now We Know

When you run a comb through your hair, both the comb and your hair become electrically charged. When electric charges are different, they try to stick to each other. The comb and your hair have different charges, so your hair moves toward the comb. This is what happened when you rubbed the balloon against your hair. Your hair stuck to the balloon.

1 Electric charges can make small pieces of paper fly through the air toward a balloon.

- Use the hole-punch to cut 10 to 15 small circles from the sheet of paper.

- Separate the circles and spread them out on a table.

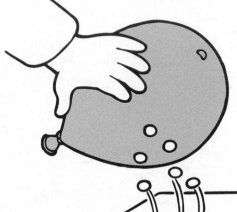

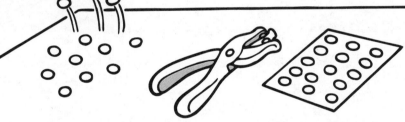

- Charge the inflated round balloon again by rubbing it on your hair as before.

- Hold the balloon close to, but not touching, the paper circles. Watch what happens to the paper circles.

2 The longer the balloon, the more surface there is that can be charged. If a balloon has a large enough charge, it can stick to a wall.

- Inflate the long balloon and charge it by rubbing it on your hair as before.

- Gently touch the charged side of the balloon against the wall, then let go. Watch what happens to the balloon.

Flashlight

round up these things

small hand towel
flashlight with 2 size D batteries
scissors
aluminum foil
ruler

later you'll need

the same materials
plus
duct tape

1 Spread the towel across a table. The towel will help prevent the flashlight parts from rolling off the table.

2 Adult Step Unscrew the bulb section of the flashlight.

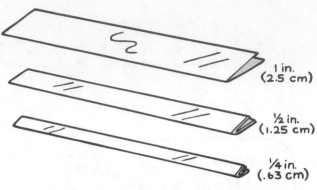

1 in. (2.5 cm)

½ in. (1.25 cm)

¼ in. (.63 cm)

3 Adult Step Remove the bulb by snapping out the plastic base that holds the bulb in place.

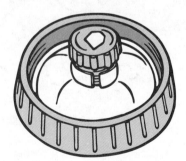

4 Remove the batteries.

5 Adult Step Cut a piece of aluminum foil 2 inches (5 cm) wide and as long as needed for the experiment.

6 Fold the foil in half lengthwise three times to make a thin strip ¼ inch (0.63 cm) wide.

7 Use the foil strip to connect the bulb to one of the batteries so that the bulb glows. NOTE: *Try to do this without looking at the drawing at the bottom of the page until after the next step.*

8 Ask a helper to hold the parts as you decide how they should be connected. If you need help, ask your helper to read the following clues one at a time:

- One end of the foil strip touches only one end of the battery.

- The other end of the foil strip wraps around the base of the bulb.

- The metal base of the bulb touches the end of the battery opposite the end the foil touches.

9 After you discover how to light the bulb, darken the room to see the light better.

So Now We Know

The bulb in a flashlight lights up when electricity flows through it. The electricity causes the wire in the bulb to get hot and glow.

More Fun Things to Know and Do

The battery pushes electricity through the foil and bulb. The amount of "push" is doubled by stacking two batteries with the "outty" and "inny" ends together. NOTE: *Stacking more than two batteries will burn out the bulb.*

- Tape the two batteries together so that the "outty" and "inny" ends are together.

- Using the 16-inch (40-cm) foil strip, light the bulb as before.

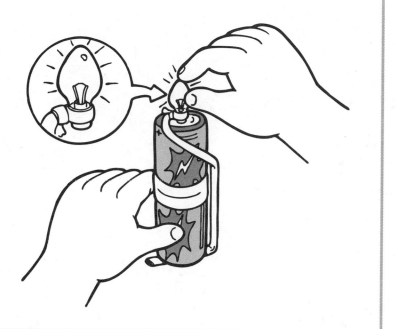

Let's find out!

Part Two   # NATURE

Basic Life-forms

Building Blocks

round up these things

cooking pot
6-ounce (170-g) package of lemon gelatin
  dessert mix
1-cup (250-ml) measuring cup
1-quart (1-liter) resealable plastic bag
2-quart (2-liter) bowl
small plum or other fruit of comparable size
5 to 6 peanuts (with or without their shells)

later you'll need

round toothpicks
modeling clay

1 **Adult Step** Using the cooking pot and gelatin dessert mix, prepare the mix according to the instructions on the box. Allow the gelatin to cool to room temperature.

2 Use the measuring cup to scoop the cooled gelatin into the resealable bag. Seal the bag and place it in the bowl.

3 Set the bowl with the bag in the refrigerator to chill until the gelatin is firm (about 3 to 4 hours).

4 Remove the bowl from the refrigerator.

5 Using your finger, insert a plum into the center of the gelatin.

6 Use your finger to insert the peanuts in the gelatin.

7 Seal the bag.

8 Hold the bag over the bowl as you gently squeeze the bag. (The bowl is used in case you squeeze too hard and the bag opens.) Observe the shape of the bag. Set the bag on a table and observe the shape of the bag. Then, pick it up and look at the shape again.

9 Put the bag in the refrigerator until it is needed for the experiment "Stiff."

So Now We Know

Cells are the building blocks of all living things. The bag of gelatin represents a model of an animal cell. It has a thin, flexible lining which holds the cell parts (the bag), the jellylike fluid that the cell parts float in (the gelatin), the control center (the plum), and the power stations where food is changed into energy (the peanuts). Like the cell model, animal cells are soft and get squeezed out of shape when something pushes against them. This change is not permanent, as you observed when you placed the bag on the table. A cat is soft because of its soft cells, but its fur also makes it feel soft.

I wonder...
If cats are made of soft cells, how can they stand up?

Bones are made of cells, but they have rocklike stuff between them that makes them hard. Show how bones give cats their shape.

- Use the toothpicks for bones and the clay for the softer cells of the body.

- Mold the clay around the toothpicks into the shape of a cat.

Stiff

round up these things

bag of gelatin and bowl from "Building Blocks"
4 to 6 green grapes
small shoe box with a lid

later you'll need

2 small bowls
tap water
knife (to be used only by an adult)
cutting board
cucumber

1 Use your finger to insert the grapes in the bag of gelatin.

2 Hold the bag over the bowl as you gently squeeze the bag. (The bowl is used in case you squeeze too hard and the bag opens.)

3 Set the bag of gelatin in the shoe box and close the lid.

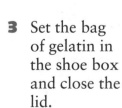

4 Hold the shoe box and gently squeeze it.

So Now We Know

Plants, like animals, are made of cells. The bag of gelatin and the shoe box represent a model of a plant cell. Plants and animals have some cell parts that are the same. But two plant cell parts that animals don't have are green food factories (the grapes) and a stiff covering around the cell (the shoe box). Plants do not have bones to give them shape. Instead, the firm cell covering helps to do this.

Water inside plant cells also makes a plant firm. Vegetables that are kept in a container of water stay crisp because water fills the cells. Show this by testing cucumber slices in and out of water.

- Fill one of the bowls half full with water.

- **Adult Step**   Use the knife and cutting board to slice the cucumber.

- Place half the cucumber slices in each bowl.

- Allow the bowls to stand undisturbed for one day.

- Remove the cucumber slices from each bowl and break each in half by bending it with your hands. Determine which cucumbers are firmer, the ones that were in the water or the ones that were not.

Predators and Prey

Blending

I wonder...
Why are some animals hard to see?

Let's find out!

round up these things

3 sheets of construction paper: 1 green,
 1 brown, 1 pale blue
pencil
scissors
ruler
glue
crayons
cotton ball

later you'll need

2 sheets of construction paper: 1 white,
 1 brown
pencil
scissors

1 Lay the green paper on top of the brown paper.

2 On one of the shorter edges of the green paper, mark and cut a 2-inch-(5-cm)-wide strip, making sure to cut through both sheets of paper.

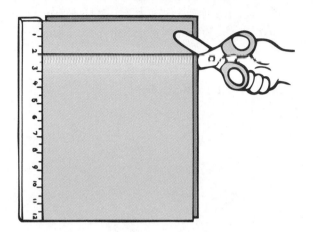

3 Glue the two paper strips together, back to back. Set them aside and allow the glue to dry.

4 Fold what's left of the stacked sheets of green and brown paper in half lengthwise (long end to long end).

5 Draw 3 blades of grass on the folded sheets of paper as shown.

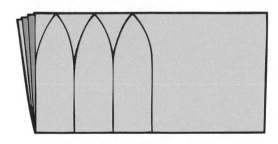

6 **Adult Step** Cut out each blade, making sure to cut through all four layers of paper and across the fold. You will have 6 blades of each color.

7 Place all 12 blades of grass along one of the longer edges of the blue paper.

Alternate the colors, placing 3 blades of one color together as shown. Glue the blades of grass to the blue paper.

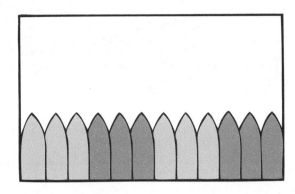

8 Complete the picture by using crayons to add a sun and birds. Separate the fibers of the cotton ball and glue it on the blue paper to represent a cloud.

9 Fold the glued strip prepared in step 3 in half lengthwise. Make a mark in the center of the strip to divide it in half. Draw two half chameleons on the fold of the strip, one on either side of the mark, as shown.

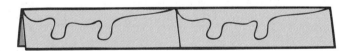

10 **Adult Step** Cut out the chameleons, making sure to cut through both thicknesses of the glued strip.

11 Place the chameleons green side up on the green grass blades. Observe how well you can see the green chameleons.

12 Turn the chameleons over, brown side up, and place them on the brown grass blades. Again observe how well you can see the brown chameleons.

13 Turn one chameleon over, green side up, and leave it on the brown grass. Which chameleon is easier to see?

So Now We Know

Some animals can change color. When an animal's color blends in with its surroundings, the animal is hard to see. This makes it hard for the animal's enemies to see it. The chameleon is a lizard that can change its skin color to different shades of green, yellow, and brown, which is the same color as the grass, branches, and soil where it lives. The paper chameleons you made were hard to see against the paper grass of the same color.

More Fun Things to Know and Do

The fur of some rabbits is white during the snowy winter months and changes to brown during the warm months. This allows the rabbit to blend in with its surroundings. Make paper rabbits and decide which would blend in with your outdoor surroundings.

- Use the papers to make one white and one brown rabbit.

- Take the rabbits outdoors and place them on different surfaces. Decide which rabbit blends in better with your outdoor surroundings.

- Test them again later when the season changes and your outdoor surroundings change.

Bright Eyes

round up these things

chalk
ruler
black construction paper
scissors
empty coffee can (inside bottom must be
  shiny)
rubber band
flashlight

later you'll need

mirror
timer

1. With the chalk, draw an oval about 3 inches (7.5 cm) long and 1 inch (2.5 cm) wide in the center of the paper.

2. Cut the oval out of the paper. Discard the oval cutout.

3. Place the paper over the open end of the can so that the oval hole in the paper is in the center of the can's opening. Secure the paper to the can with the rubber band.

4. Take the can and the flashlight to a room that you can make very dark, and turn out the lights.

5. Hold the can in front of you as far away as you can at eye level so that the hole in the paper faces you.

6. Look toward the hole in the paper. You will find that it is difficult or impossible to see the hole (or even the can, if the room is very dark).

7. Hold the flashlight near your face so that the light points at the hole in the paper.

8 Look toward the hole in the paper. The light from the flashlight will reflect off the shiny bottom of the can, making the hole appear to glow.

So Now We Know

The glow from a cat's eyes is light that has entered through the opening in the eye and bounced off the shiny mirrorlike lining at the back of the eye. This special lining helps the cat see better at night so that it can more easily find food.

More Fun Things to Know and Do

The pupil is a black opening in the center of the eye of cats and other animals, such as humans. It enlarges in the dark so that more light can get into the eye. To make your pupil get larger, keep one eye open and the other eye closed. Use your hand to cover the closed eye. Observe the size of the pupil of the open eye by looking in the mirror. At the end of 2 to 3 minutes, remove your hand, open the closed eye, and look at it in the mirror. Watch what happens to the size of the pupil in the light.

Body Temperature

Chill Out

small bowl
tap water
cotton ball
ruler

the same materials
plus
bulb-type thermometer
timer

1 Fill the bowl about half full with water.

2 Dip the cotton ball into the water in the bowl and squeeze out any excess water.

3 Rub the wet cotton ball over the surface of your arm.

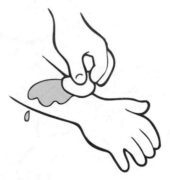

4 Hold your wet arm about 4 inches (10 cm) from your mouth.

5 Blow across the wet area on your arm. How does your arm feel?

So Now We Know

A dog does not sweat like you do when it gets hot. Instead, it pants by blowing its breath over its wet tongue. This helps the dog cool off, just as your arm felt cooler after you wet it and blew your breath across it.

More Fun Things to Know and Do

A thermometer is an instrument that measures changes in temperature. Let's use a thermometer to show the change in temperature that happens when you blow on something wet.

- Lay the thermometer on a table. Observe the level of the liquid line in the thermometer.

- Moisten the cotton ball with water. Separate the fibers of the cotton ball and lay a thin layer of wet cotton across the bulb of the thermometer.

- Keeping your mouth about 4 inches (10 cm) away from the wet cotton, blow your breath across the wet

cotton about 15 times. Observe the level of the liquid line in the thermometer again. If the line goes up, it indicates an increase in temperature. If the line goes down, it indicates a decrease in temperature.

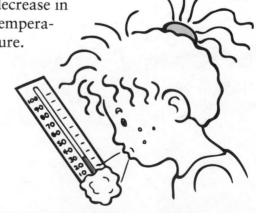

Overcoats

round up these things

wool glove
2 ice cubes

later you'll need

1 tablespoon (15 ml) vegetable shortening
two 1-quart (1-liter) plastic bags
2 ice cubes

1 Put the glove on your hand.

2 Hold one ice cube in the gloved hand and the other ice cube in your other hand for about 5 seconds. Measure 5 seconds by counting to 5, saying "one thousand" before each number (one thousand one, one thousand two, and so on). Notice how cold the ice makes each hand feel.

So Now We Know

Animals don't have overcoats to put on when it is cold. Instead they have a permanent coat of fur or feathers that they wear all year long. The coat gets thicker during the winter. The wool glove, like the fur or feathers on an animal, protects against the cold. The skin on your hand, like the skin on an animal, is a waterproof covering but doesn't offer much protection against the cold.

More Fun Things to Know and Do

Some animals that live in very cold places, such as walruses, seals, and whales, have a thick layer of blubber (fat) under their skin. Let's see how this fatty layer helps to keep them warm.

- Place the shortening in your left hand.

- Place your hand inside the bag. The plastic bag represents the skin on an animal, and the shortening represents the layer of fat beneath the skin.

- Cup your shortening-covered hand and place the ice cube on top of the plastic bag.

- Place your other hand inside the other plastic bag. Cup your hand and place the other ice cube on top of this plastic bag.

- Hold the ice in your hands for about 5 seconds. Compare how cold each hand feels.

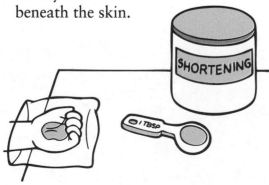

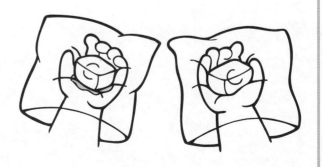

Animal Movement

Glider

round up these things

sheet of typing paper
marking pen
scissors
2 paper clips

later you'll need

the same materials

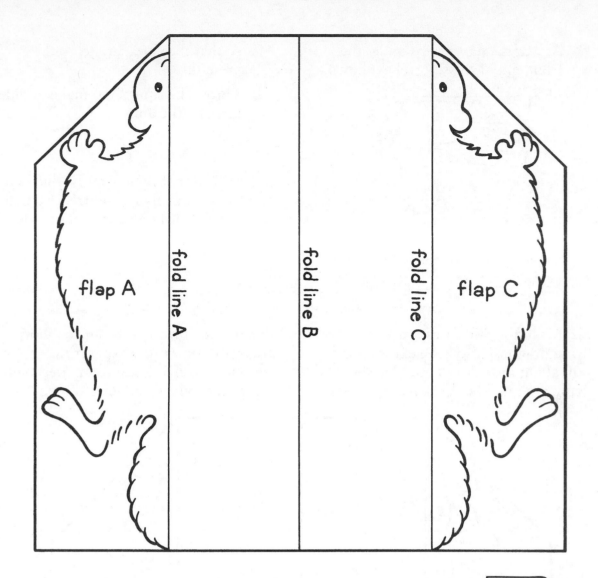

1. Lay the paper over the flying squirrel pattern.

2. Trace all the outlines and fold lines.

3. Cut around the outlines of the traced drawing.

4. Fold the paper in half along fold line B so that the drawings on flaps A and C touch.

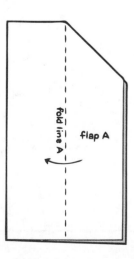

5. Fold flap A along fold line A and toward the first fold.

6. Turn the paper over, then fold flap C along fold line C and toward the first fold.

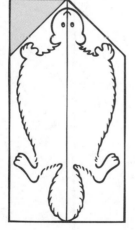

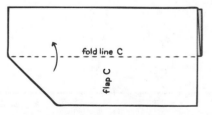

7 Attach the paper clips under the front end of the squirrel as shown.

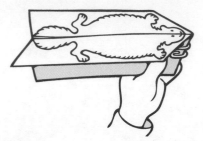

8 Holding the squirrel from below (fold line B), adjust the flaps so that they are parallel to the ground.

9 Throw the squirrel to make it glide through the air.

So Now We Know

Squirrels cannot fly like birds. But some squirrels, called flying squirrels, can glide through the air like your paper model when they leap from one branch to another.

More Fun Things to Know and Do

Lizards in the rain forest of Asia, called flying dragons, also have extra flaps of skin along the sides of their bodies. The flying dragon, like the flying squirrel, is able to glide through the air for short distances. Repeat the experiment, replacing the flying squirrel pattern with that of the flying dragon as shown.

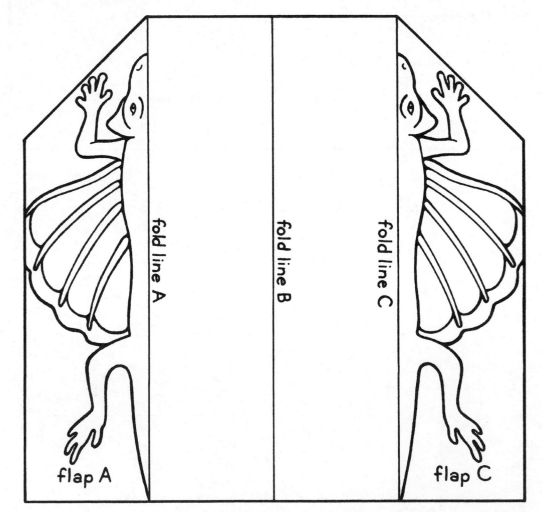

Floaters

large bowl
tap water
2 glass marbles
two 7-inch (17.5-cm) round balloons

4 to 5 fast-food condiment packets
   (ketchup, mayonnaise, soy sauce, etc.)
1-quart (1-liter) jar
tap water
2-liter plastic soda bottle with cap

1 Fill the bowl about three-fourths full with water.

2 Place 1 marble inside each balloon.

3 In one of the balloons, tie a knot as close to the marble as possible.

4 Slightly inflate the second balloon, and tie a knot as close to the mouth of the balloon as possible.

5 Drop both of the balloons in the bowl of water. The inflated balloon will float on the surface of the water,

but the deflated balloon will sink to the bottom of the bowl.

So Now We Know

Fish do not have marbles inside them. The marble is used to make the balloon heavy. Fish do have a special organ inside them that works like a balloon. Like the balloons in the experiment, as the amount of air inside the fish's organ increases, the fish rises to the surface. As the amount of air decreases, the fish sinks.

More Fun Things to Know and Do

Here is another way to demonstrate the rising and sinking of a fish.

- Decide which of the condiment packets will make the best model of a fish. Do this by filling the jar about three-fourths full with water and dropping all of the packets into the water. The best fish model is the packet that just barely sinks below the waters surface.

- Fill the soda bottle to overflowing with water.

- Insert the selected condiment packet in the bottle. Add water if necessary

so that the bottle is still overflowing with water.

- Secure the cap on the bottle.

- Squeeze the bottle with your hands. The air bubble in the packet will shrink and the model fish will sink.

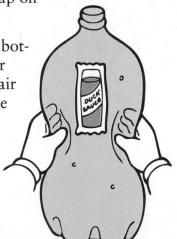

- Release the pressure on the bottle. The air bubble inside the packet will get bigger and the model fish will rise.

Plant Growth

Sprouters

round up these things

large 1-tablespoon (15-ml) measuring
  spoon
12-ounce (260-ml) paper cup
potting soil
5 dry beans, such as pinto or lima
pencil
saucer
tap water

later you'll need

paper towels
10-ounce (300-ml) clear plastic cup
tap water
seeds from the kitchen, such as popcorn,
  dill, celery, mustard, peppercorns, fennel,
  or whole cloves
masking tape
marking pen

1 Use the spoon to fill the paper cup three-fourths full with soil.

2 Place the beans on the surface of the soil.

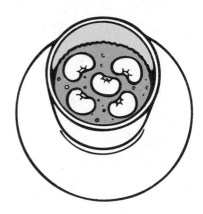

3 Cover the beans with 4 tablespoons (60 ml) of soil.

4 **Adult Step** Use the pencil to punch four or five holes around the bottom edge of the cup.

5 Set the cup in the saucer.

6 Moisten the soil with water. Keep the soil moist, but not soggy, during the experiment.

7 Place the cup and saucer near a window that receives sunlight at least part of the day. The light from the sun will keep the soil warm.

8 Watch the surface of the soil for signs of growth. It may take 4 to 6 days for the sprouting beans to break through the soil. Look first for a hook-shaped stem to break through the surface. As the hook straightens, leaves on the end of the stem will be lifted up.

9 Continue to watch the growth of the beans for 2 to 3 weeks or longer.

So Now We Know

The dry beans in your kitchen are the seeds of a bean plant. The beans will grow if they are planted and given the right amount of light, water, air, and warmth. Beans that have been cooked will not grow because the heat kills the seed. Sometimes a bean doesn't grow because an injury has caused some of its parts to be damaged or missing.

Not all of the seeds that you find in your kitchen will grow. Many have been heated or injured in other ways. Plant other seeds found in the kitchen to see whether they will grow.

- Prepare a see-through growing cup by folding a paper towel in half and lining the inside of the plastic cup with it.

- Crumple other paper towels and stuff them into the cup to hold the paper lining tightly against the sides of the cup.

- Moisten the paper lining with water. Keep the lining moist, but not soggy, during the experiment.

- Take a few of one kind of seed and slip each seed between the paper lining and the cup. Leave space between the seeds, but group seeds of the same type in one section of the cup.

- Take a few of another kind of seed and slip each seed between the paper lining and the cup in another section of the cup.

- Place a strip of tape around the outside of the cup. Write the name of each kind of seed on the tape.

- See which of your seeds will grow.

Sun Seekers

masking tape
small potted houseplant, such as ivy, coleus,
  or spathiphyllum
marking pen
NOTE: *This experiment works best in a
room that receives most of its light from a
window.*

sunflower growing outdoors
compass

1 Place a small piece of tape on either side of the flowerpot.

2 Mark a dot on one piece of tape and an X on the other piece.

3 Set the plant near a window that receives direct sunlight. Turn the pot so that the X faces the window.

4 Observe the direction of the leaves every day for 1 week or longer. NOTE: *Water the plant as usual.*

5 Repeat steps 3 and 4, turning the pot so that the dot on the tape faces the window. Notice any change in the direction of the leaves.

So Now We Know

The leaves on the plant move toward the window. When the plant is turned around, the leaves again move toward the window. This happens because the plant's stems grow toward the light. As the plant stems grow, the leaves are turned toward the light.

I wonder...
Does a sunflower always face the sun?

Sunflowers face the sun during the day. To do this, they turn during the day to follow the sun from east to west. Observe this by doing the following:

- Find a sunflower growing outdoors.

- Several times during the day, use the compass to determine the direction that the sunflower is facing. CAUTION: *Do not look at the sun. It can damage your eyes.*

85

Plant Parts

Juicy

manila file folder
ruler
transparent tape
1-gallon (4-liter) plastic produce bag
1-quart (1-liter) pitcher
tap water

scissors
dishwashing sponge
2 saucers
petroleum jelly
½ cup (125 ml) tap water

1 Fold the folder like a fan, beginning at one of the short ends. Make each fold about 1 inch (2.5 cm) wide.

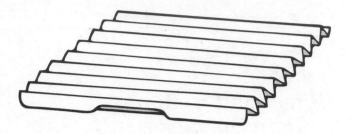

2 Bring the two ends of the folder together to make a cylinder. Secure the ends with tape.

3 Insert the plastic bag in the cylinder. Fold the open end of the bag down over the top of the cylinder.

4 Squeeze the folds together to make a narrow cylinder. Stand the cylinder on a table so that the open end of the plastic bag is at the top.

5 Fill the pitcher with water.

6 Hold the cylinder upright on the table as your helper slowly pours the water from the pitcher into the plastic bag.

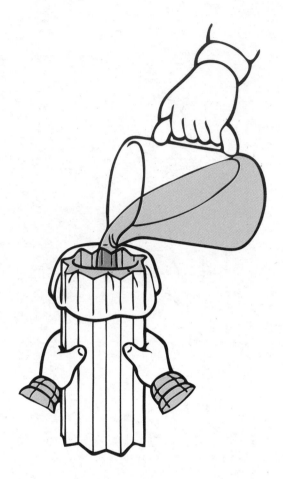

7 Observe the cylinder as the water enters the bag.

So Now We Know

The outsides of some cacti are pleated like the cylinder. This allows them to swell with water during rainy periods, just as your cylinder swelled with water. This water is used by the cactus when it doesn't rain.

All plants lose water through their leaves and stems. The leaves of many desert plants have a thick, waxy coat. See how this coat makes it harder for the plants to lose water.

- **Adult Step** Cut the sponge in half.

- Lay one half of the sponge in one of the saucers.

- Cover all but one of the larger surfaces of the other half of the sponge with a thick layer of petroleum jelly.

- Lay the greased sponge, ungreased side down, in the second saucer.

- Pour half of the water into each saucer. When both sponges have soaked up the water, pour out the excess water from the saucers.

- Once a day, touch the undersides of the sponge pieces to see whether they are wet. How long does it take them to dry? Which sponge dries out first?

Browning

I wonder... Why do peeled bananas turn brown?

Let's find out!

round up these things

2 bananas
paper plate
butter knife

later you'll need

chewable vitamin C tablet
paper towel
rolling pin
paring knife (to be used only by an adult)
apple
2 paper plates
lemon
timer

1 Peel one banana and place it on the paper plate.

2 Use the butter knife to cut the banana into four sections.

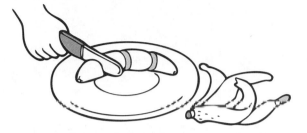

3 Look at the banana slices as often as possible during the day. You will find that the outside of each banana slice slowly turns darker.

4 After 4 to 5 hours or longer, peel the second banana and use the butter knife to cut it into four sections.

5 Compare the color of the two sectioned bananas.

So Now We Know

Bananas are protected by their skins. When the skin is peeled off, air touches the banana and it turns brown.

More Fun Things to Know and Do

Other fruits, such as apples and pears, also turn dark when their protective skin is broken or removed. Vitamin C can be used to help keep the fruit from turning dark.

- Wrap the vitamin C tablet in the paper towel and crush it by rolling the rolling pin back and forth across the towel.

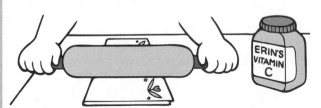

- **Adult Step** Use the paring knife to cut an unpeeled apple in half. Place the sections on separate plates.

- **Adult Step** Cut one of the sections in half.

- Sprinkle the crushed vitamin C tablet over the surface of one of the smaller sections.

- **Adult Step** Cut the lemon in half.

- Squeeze the juice from one of the lemon halves over the surface of the second small section. *NOTE: Lemons contain vitamin C.*

- Compare the color of the surfaces of the three apple sections after they have been exposed to the air for one hour or more.

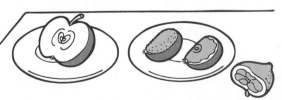

Flowers

Scented

round up these things

baby food jar (or any small jar) with lid
2 cups (500 ml) petals of roses or other
  scented flower (collected from garden
  plants)
rubbing alcohol (to be used only by an
  adult)
NOTE: *Get an adult's permission before
collecting flower petals.*

later you'll need

the remaining petals from the original
  experiment
        plus
12-inch (30-cm)-square piece of netting
rubber band
1-yard (1-m) string

1 Fill the jar with the flower petals. NOTE: *Keep the remaining flower petals for the experiment in "More Fun Things to Know and Do."*

2 **Adult Step** Fill the jar with the rubbing alcohol. Secure the lid.

3 Set the jar aside for 7 or more days.

4 After 7 or more days, open the jar. With you finger, dab a few drops of the liquid on your wrist. CAUTION: *Keep the alcohol away from your nose and mouth.*

5 Allow the liquid to dry, then smell your wrist.

So Now We Know

Flowers smell nice because of oils in their petals. The sweet-smelling oils in the flower petals dissolved in the alcohol. When you dabbed the liquid on your skin, the alcohol evaporated, leaving a pleasant scent on your skin.

The smell of scented oils in flower petals attracts bees and other insects to the flower. Show how scented flowers attract insects. NOTE: *This experiment works best during warm seasons.*

- Pour the flower petals remaining from the experiment into the center of the netting.

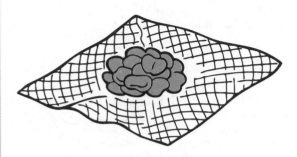

- Wrap the netting around the petals, forming a bag of petals. Secure the bag with the rubber band.

- Tie one end of the string around the top of the bag of petals to close the bag.

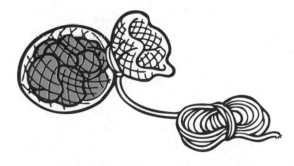

- Choose an outdoor place visible through a window from which you can make frequent observations of

the bag. This could be a tree limb outside a window near the kitchen table or your desk, or if no tree limb is available, the window frame itself.

- **Adult Step** Hang the bag of petals in the chosen spot.

- Observe the bag of petals for 2 or more days. Use an insect field guide to help you identify the insects that visit the bag.

- At the end of the experiment, the bag of petals can be hung in your room to give the room a sweet smell. CAUTION: *Make sure there aren't any insects still on or in the bag before you bring it indoors.*

Keepers

round up these things

6-inch (15-cm)-square sheet of black
  construction paper
pencil
ruler
scissors
6-inch (15-cm)-square sheet of waxed paper
two 6-inch (15-cm)-square sheets of clear
  Contact paper
plant sample (flowers and leaves of a small
  flowering plant, such as four-o'clocks or
  clover)

one-hole paper punch
6-inch (15-cm) piece of string
small suction cup with hook (used to secure
  hanging crafts to windowpanes)

later you'll need

the same materials
    but
substitute flower with petals, such as a
  sunflower, for small flowering plant
    plus
permanent marker

1 Fold the black paper in half.

2 Draw a 2-by-4-inch (5-by-10-cm) rectangle on the fold.

3 Cut out and discard the rectangle. Unfold the paper. You have made a frame.

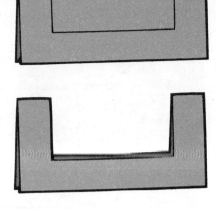

4 Place the frame on top of the waxed paper.

5 **Adult Step** Remove the backing from one piece of Contact paper and place it over the frame.

6 Turn the frame over and remove the waxed paper to expose the sticky surface of the Contact paper.

7 Arrange the flower parts on the sticky surface of the Contact paper.

8 **Adult Step** Remove the backing from the second piece of Contact paper and place it over the flowers and frame.

9 Use scissors to trim away any Contact paper that might extend past the edges of the frame.

10 Make a hole in the center top of the frame with the paper punch.

11 Thread the string through the hole in the frame and tie the ends together.

12 Attach the suction cup to a window.

13 Hang the frame on the suction cup hook.

So Now We Know

As fresh flowers and other plant parts get older, they dry and lose their shape. Sandwiching the flower parts between layers of sticky paper helps prevent the plant parts from losing their shape.

Plant parts can be used to create your own design. A flower design can be made as follows:

- Repeat steps 1 to 6 of the original experiment.

- Use the marker to draw a face on the sticky surface of the Contact paper.

- Place the flower petals and leaves around the face, as shown.

- **Adult Step** Remove the backing from the second piece of Contact paper and place it over the flowers and frame.

- Repeat steps 9 to 13 to finish your picture.

Let's find out!

Part Three BUGS

Collecting

Trapper

round up these things

pencil
ruler
3-by-5-inch (7.5-by-12.5-cm) index card
scissors
12-inch (30-cm) white chenille craft
  stem (available at craft stores) or pipe
  cleaner
school glue
3 miniature marshmallows
black felt-tip pen
round toothpick

10-ounce (300-ml) clear plastic cup
4-by-6-inch (10-by-15-cm) index card
magnifying lens
friend

later you'll need

insect and collecting cup from original
  experiment
pencil
1-quart (1-liter) resealable plastic bag
6-by-8-inch (15-by-20-cm) index card
magnifying lens

1 Draw a line about ½ inch (1.25 cm) from the short end of the smaller index card.

2 Cut along the line to make a paper strip.

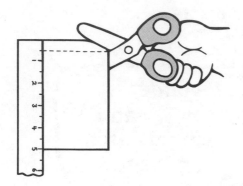

3 **Adult Step** Cut a 1-inch (2.5-cm) piece from the end of the craft stem. Push the piece of craft stem through the 3 marshmallows so they are joined end to end to form the body of an insect.

4 Glue the center marshmallow to the middle of the paper strip as shown. Allow the glue to dry. This will take about 5 to 10 minutes.

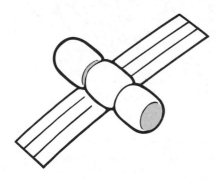

5 **Adult Step** Draw two lines on each side of the paper from the outer end toward the marshmallow, dividing each side into three equal parts.

6 Cut along the lines.

7 Bend the paper strips to form six legs.

8 Use the pen to draw two eyes on one of the end marshmallows. This marshmallow will be the insect's head.

9 **Adult Step** Break off about ½ inch (1.25 cm) from both ends of the toothpick. Discard the center of the toothpick.

10 Insert the pointed ends of the toothpick pieces into the head to make two antennae.

11 Set the insect on a table. Push the remaining, long piece of craft stem into the hind end of the insect. Have your friend hold the craft stem and make the insect slowly move around.

12 Catch the insect by quickly, but gently, turning the plastic cup over the insect. This cup will be called the catching cup. Be careful not to "injure" the insect.

13 Have your friend hold the insect in place with the catching cup while you pull out the craft stem.

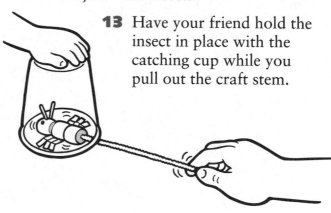

14 Carefully slide the larger index card under the cup and the insect without giving the insect enough room to "sneak out."

15 Use the magnifying lens to study your insect.

So Now We Know

You can catch real insects the same way that you caught your pretend insect. Using the catching cup and a magnifying lens, you can study insects up close without touching them. When you are done, just pick up the cup and let the insect walk or fly away.

More Fun Things to Know and Do

To study an insect more closely, you can move it to a plastic bag. Here's how to move an insect from the catching cup to a holding bag:

- **Adult Step** Use the pencil to make five or six small airholes through the plastic bag near the top so the insect from the original experiment has air to "breathe." This bag will be called the holding bag.

- Hold the bag open while your friend dumps the insect from the collecting cup into the holding bag.

- Lay the index card on a table near a window or lamp.

- Place the holding bag with the insect on the card.

- Hold the insect stationary by gently pressing the bag next to its body. Then, use the magnifying lens to study the insect. Be careful not to squeeze the insect and "hurt" it.

Now you are ready to catch a real insect. Remember not to leave a live insect in the holding bag too long. After about 30 minutes, return the insect to where you found it. *CAUTION: Never touch an insect unless you know that it will not harm you.*

Bug House

round up these things

2 cups (500 ml) dry sand or soil
1-gallon (4-liter) wide-mouthed jar
empty toilet tissue tube
scissors
dishwashing sponge
lid from a small jar
tap water
2 or 3 twigs that will fit inside the jar

2 tablespoons (30 ml) dry cereal
slice of raw apple
5 to 6 crickets (caught or purchased from
  a pet store)
knee-high stocking

later you'll need

your crickets from original experiment

1 Pour the sand into the jar.

2 Put the tube in the jar for the crickets to have a place to hide.

3 **Adult Step** Cut a round piece of sponge that will fit inside the lid.

4 Moisten the sponge with water, set it in the lid, and place the lid inside the jar. The crickets will drink the water from the sponge, so be sure to keep it moist while you have your crickets.

5 Add the twigs to the jar. The crickets will climb on the twigs.

6 Drop the cereal and the apple slice into the jar. The crickets will eat this food, so add more when it is gone.

7 Place your crickets in the jar and immediately cover the opening with the stocking. The stocking allows air in but keeps the crickets from escaping.

8 Observe the crickets inside their house as often as possible for 1 to 2 weeks, then release them outdoors.

So Now We Know

You have made a house that crickets can live in. Watch your crickets as they eat, drink, and move around their home.

More Fun Things to Know and Do

Just for fun, you can name your crickets. To name a cricket, you need to know if it is a boy or a girl. This can be done by looking at its hind end. All crickets have two feelers on their hind end, but the female has a third tube that looks like a stinger. It's not a stinger, it's an egg-laying tube. Study the pictures of boy and girl crickets shown here to tell which of your crickets are boys and which are girls.

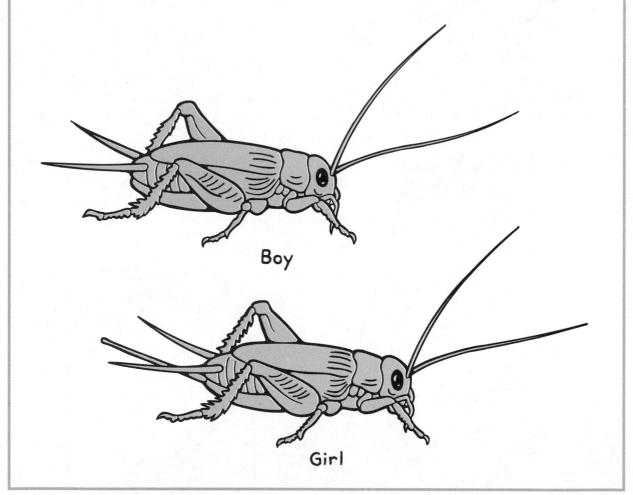

Boy

Girl

Changing

Around and Around

Nursery

Let's find out!

I wonder... Where do butterflies come from?

round up these things

6-inch (15-cm) circle of blue construction paper
black marking pen
school glue
white paper plate
3-inch (7.5-cm) square of red construction paper
scissors

6-inch (15-cm) black chenille craft stem (available at craft stores) or pipe cleaner
3-by-4-inch (7.5-by-10-cm) piece of green construction paper
7 to 10 uncooked grains of rice
three ½-inch (1.25-cm) craft pom-poms (Iridescent ones work best.)
3-inch (7.5-cm) twig
12 inches (30 cm) of masking tape

6-inch (15-cm) circle of blue construction
  paper
black marking pen
school glue
white paper plate
pencil
2 crayons, green and brown
7 to 10 uncooked grains of rice

1 Fold the blue paper circle in half
twice to divide the circle into four
equal pie slices.

2 Unfold the paper and use the pen to
draw a line along each fold line.

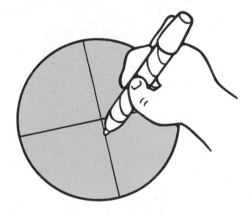

3 Glue the blue circle to the center of
the paper plate.

4 Fold the red
square in half
and draw a
wing shape as
shown in the
picture.

5 **Adult Step**
Cut out the
wings by cut-
ting through
both layers
of paper.

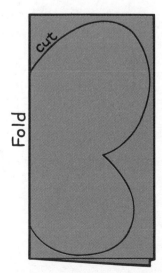

6 Unfold the wings and use the pen to
decorate the wings of the butterfly.
Make the decorations on the left
wings match those on the right
wings.

7 Fold the craft stem in half and slip
the center of the wings into the
folded stem. The stem represents the
butterfly's body. Twist the stem
together to hold the body in place,
then flare the ends of the stem out-
ward to make antennae.

8 Glue the butterfly to one of the sections of the blue circle. This is the
adult butterfly. Write ADULT on the
plate.

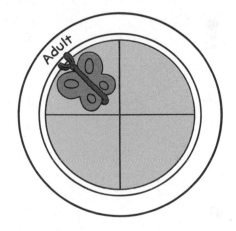

9 Cut 2 leaves from the green paper.

10 Glue one leaf to the section to the
right of the butterfly. Glue the rice
grains to this leaf. The rice represents
the eggs laid by the adult on the leaf.
Write EGGS on the plate.

11 Tear a small piece out of the remaining leaf. Glue the leaf to the next
section on the plate. Then, glue the
pom-poms to the leaf. The pom-
poms represent a caterpillar that has
hatched from one of the eggs and is
eating the leaf. Write CATERPILLAR on
the plate.

12 Glue the twig to the last section. Roll the masking tape into a small tube-like shape and glue it next to the twig. The tape represents a chrysalis, the resting stage during which a caterpillar changes into an adult. Write CHRYSALIS on the plate.

13 Draw arrows between the sections on the blue paper as shown.

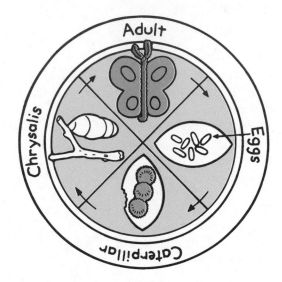

14 Rotate the plate counterclockwise and see the changes a butterfly goes through.

So Now We Know

The butterfly growth wheel shows an adult butterfly laying eggs. One of the eggs changes into a caterpillar and the caterpillar changes into a chrysalis. The chrysalis changes into another adult butterfly.

An adult grasshopper lays her eggs in the ground. The eggs change into small grasshoppers called nymphs. The nymphs grow into adult grasshoppers. Using the procedure from the original experiment, make a grasshopper growth wheel by dividing the paper plate into three sections. Use the pencil to draw the different changes of the grasshopper as shown in the pictures here. Use the pen to label the changes. Color the grass green and the grasshopper brown. Glue the grains of rice to the egg section. Draw arrows between the sections as shown. Rotate the plate to see how a grasshopper grows up.

Break Out

round up these things

newspaper
transparent tape
cookie

later you'll need

sleeping bag
2 matching scarves

1 Stand with your arms folded over your chest.

2 **Adult Step** Wrap two layers of newspaper around the child's body, one layer around her chest and the other around her hips. Use tape to secure the papers together.

3 **Adult Step** Hold the cookie to the child's mouth so she can take a bite.

4 Eat the bite of cookie, and then pretend to grow by spreading your arms and pushing out on the paper. The paper around your chest will tear apart, but the paper around your hips will stay together.

5 Allow the paper to fall, then step out of the paper and leave it on the floor.

So Now We Know

Young grasshoppers eat and grow larger, but their outer covering, called an exoskeleton, does not grow. When a grasshopper's exoskeleton gets too tight, this covering splits and the grasshopper wiggles out just as you did when you broke out of the paper. The grasshopper has a new, larger exoskeleton underneath the old one.

Some insects, such as butterflies, do not grow from smaller versions of themselves. Instead the butterfly grows by changing shape and form entirely. (See the experiment "Around and Around" for more on butterfly growth.) A special sac called a chrysalis forms around a caterpillar. The butterfly that emerges from the chrysalis is at its adult size. Here's a way to show these changes:

- Lay an open sleeping bag on the floor.

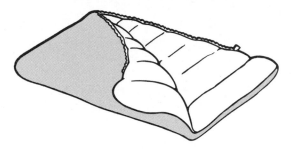

- Place the scarves inside the bag.

- Pretend to be a caterpillar and crawl inside the bag. Zip the bag closed over your body. The bag is your chrysalis.

- Inside the chrysalis, a caterpillar changes into a butterfly with wings.

- Find the scarves, and hold one in each hand. The scarves are your wings.

- During the change from a caterpillar to a butterfly, little or no movement inside the chrysalis is seen. Lie very still for a few seconds, and then unzip the bag.

- At first, emerging butterflies are wet and need time to dry. Slowly crawl out, stand, and walk around very slowly with your arms and the scarf wings hanging by your body. Then, start flapping your wings as you pretend to be a flying butterfly.

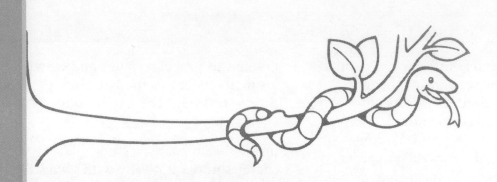

Moving

Creepers

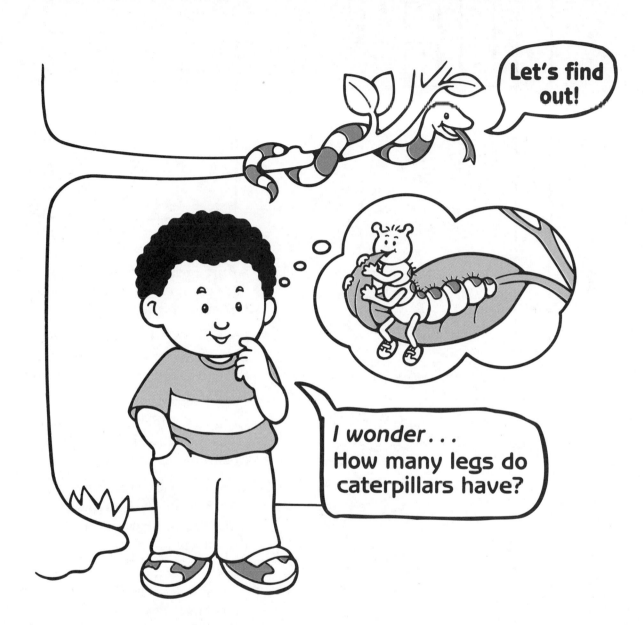

1-by-11-inch (2.5-by-27.5-cm) strip of
  typing paper
scissors
black marking pen
ruler

no. 10 crochet thread
4-ply knitting yarn
transparent tape

caterpillar made in original experiment

1 Fold the paper in half four times, with the short ends together. Unfold the paper.

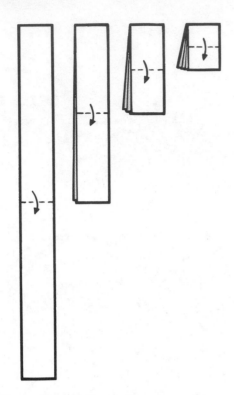

2 Cut off and discard two sections of one end of the strip.

3 Refold the strip, making accordion folds along the length of the paper.

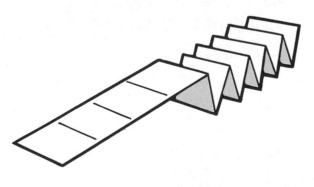

4 With the strip completely folded, draw two curved lines and 12 dots on one end section as shown. This section will be the caterpillar's head. The 12 dots represent eyes, 6 on each side of the head.

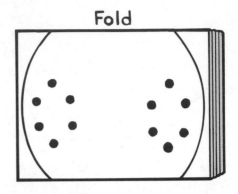

5 Adult Step Cut along both curved lines drawn on the paper, cutting through all layers of the paper.

6 Stretch the paper out. Starting with the segment next to the head, number the body segments from 1 through 13.

7 Cut three 2-inch (5-cm) pieces of crochet thread and five 1¼-inch (3-cm) pieces of yarn.

8 Tape a thread across each of the first three body segments. These threads represent the true legs of the caterpillar.

9 Tape the yarn across segments 6, 7, 8, 9, and 13. The thick yarn represents false legs.

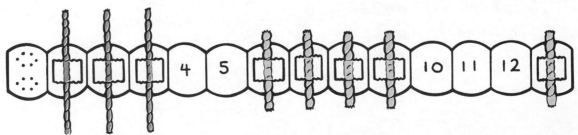

So Now We Know

Most caterpillars have 16 legs: 6 long, thin, true legs; and 10 shorter, fatter, false legs. The true legs will become the legs of the adult butterfly or moth. The false legs will disappear.

More Fun Things to Know and Do

1 Caterpillars move by drawing the hind pair of false legs forward. These legs then hold on to the surface as the next pair of legs moves forward. Each pair of legs moves forward, one after the other. The caterpillar's body moves in a wavelike motion. Use the paper caterpillar from the original experiment to show how a caterpillar moves.

- Refold your caterpillar and place it on a flat surface, such as a table.

- Hold the head segment in one hand and the hind segment in the other hand.

- Push the hind segment forward, moving the body segments closer together.

- Pull the head segment forward, moving the body segments farther apart. Your caterpillar shows how a real caterpillar moves.

2 Catch a caterpillar using the instructions in the experiment "Trapper." Transfer the caterpillar to a 1-gallon (4-liter) jar that has a branch inside. Observe the movement of the caterpillar. If you wish to keep the caterpillar and watch it change into a moth or butterfly, put in the jar some of the plants the caterpillar was found eating and add more when they have been eaten. Remove the caterpillar and clean out the jar every 2 to 3 days. Use a field guide to caterpillars, such as *Peterson's First Guides to Caterpillars* by Amy Bartlett Wright (New York: Houghton Mifflin, 1993), to identify your caterpillar and find out how long it will take to make the change. See the experiment "Around and Around" for information on the different growth stages. CAUTION: *Unless you know the caterpillar is harmless, do not touch it or pick it up.*

Springy

round up these things

ruler
file folder
pencil
scissors
school glue
black marking pen

later you'll need

flea hopper made in original experiment
materials to make more flea hoppers
masking tape
small Post-it notes
black marking pen

1 Lay the ruler across the widest part of the closed file folder.

2 Use the pencil to draw two lines on the folder, one on each side of the ruler.

3 **Adult Step** Cut along both lines on the folder, cutting through both layers of the folder. Keep the two strips.

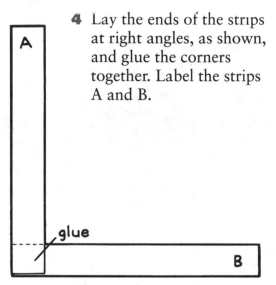

4 Lay the ends of the strips at right angles, as shown, and glue the corners together. Label the strips A and B.

5 When the glue dries, fold strip B (the bottom strip) over strip A (the top strip).

6 Repeat step 5, folding the bottom strip over the top strip, until the strips are completely folded. Glue the ends together. This paper spring will be your flea hopper.

7 Stand the flea hopper on a flat surface, such as the floor. Push the folds of the flea hopper together with one finger; then quickly slide your finger off and watch the flea hopper jump up.

So Now We Know

Before a flea jumps, the springlike material in its hind legs is pushed together, like the spring in your flea hopper. When the flea's legs stretch out again, the "springs" push the legs forward and the flea jumps through the air.

If the size of the body is considered, fleas would win the gold medal in any Olympic jumping contest. Some fleas can jump 12 inches (30 cm) or more. This is almost 200 times the flea's body length. If you could jump like a flea, you could hop over a 50-story building! Have a "flea Olympics" with the flea hopper you made in the original experiment.

- Invite friends to make flea hoppers. Experiment by using different widths and lengths of paper strips for each flea hopper.

- Test one hopper at a time. Place it on a starting line made with a piece of masking tape on the floor. Mark where the hopper first lands, using a Post-it note with the name of the person testing the hopper.

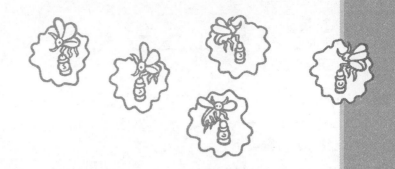

Communicating

Dancers

round up these things

7 sheets of white copy paper
7 sheets of colored copy paper (any color)
pencil
scissors
black marking pen
masking tape
candy bar
ruler

later you'll need

dance pattern made in original
  experiment
candy bar

1 Fold one white and one colored sheet of paper in half (short ends together).

2 Unfold the white paper and make an outline of your right shoe on each side of the fold line on the paper.

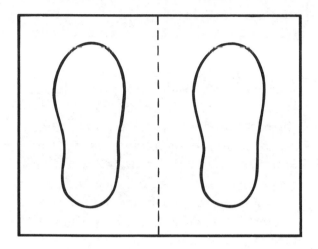

3 Repeat step 2, using the colored paper and your left shoe.

4 **Adult Step**   Stack the rest of the white papers and put the sheet with the shoe outlines on top. Cut out the 2 outlines, cutting through all seven layers.

5 **Adult Step**   Repeat step 4, using the colored papers.

6 Use the pen to number 8 of the white shoe cutouts with odd numbers from 1 through 15. Number the 6 remaining white shoe cutouts with odd numbers from 5 through 15.

7 Number 8 of the colored shoe cutouts with even numbers from 2 through 16. Number the 6 remaining colored shoe cutouts with even numbers from 6 through 16.

8 Lay the shoe cutouts on the floor in the pattern shown here. Use the tape to secure the cutouts to the floor. This is the pattern of a bee's dance.

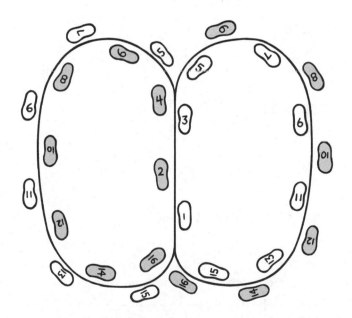

9 Place the candy bar in its wrapper on the floor in line with the center line of the dance pattern and as far as possible from the pattern.

10 Stand with your right foot on the white number 1 cutout and your left foot on the colored number 2 cutout. You will be facing in the direction of the candy bar.

11 Walk forward, placing your feet on cutouts 3 and 4. Then, step on cutout 5 on the left side of the pattern and walk around the left side and through the center. When you reach cutout 4 again, step on cutout 5 on the right and walk around the right side. Follow the path several times. You are doing a bee dance called the waggle dance.

So Now We Know

Bees tell each other where faraway food is by doing a waggle dance. (By the way, bees eat nectar from flowers, not candy bars! And all of the bees that collect nectar are female.) The bee first flies in a straight line that points toward the food. She flies in a circle around one side of the line to get back to her starting place and then retraces the straight line and flies in a circle around the other side. She moves from one side to the other, making a pattern that looks like the number 8.

The straight line through the bee's dance pattern indicates the direction of the food, but it's the movement of the bee's body along the straight line that indicates how far away the food is. To tell distance, she waggles her head and body, moving them quickly from side to side. The faster she waggles, the farther away the food is. Thus, the dance is called the waggle dance. Move through the dance pattern on the floor again, this time waggling your body as you move along the straight line. Take turns doing the waggle dance with a friend. Repeat, moving the candy bar about 1 foot (30 cm) closer to the pattern and waggling your body slower.

Flashers

I wonder... Why do fireflies light up?

Let's find out!

round up these things

empty paper towel tube

1-ounce (30-ml) light stick (available where camping supplies are sold)

later you'll need

scissors

10-by-12-inch (25-by-30-cm) sheet of brown construction paper

20-ounce (600-ml) clear straight-sided plastic bottle with lid

transparent tape

school glue

two 7-mm wiggle eyes (available at craft stores)

12-inch (30-cm) yellow chenille craft stem (available at craft stores) or pipe cleaner

pencil

activated light stick from original experiment

CAUTION: *Do not break the light stick open, because it has glass inside. The contents of light sticks are nontoxic, so the light stick may be disposed of by throwing it in the trash.*

1 Stand the paper tube on a chair. Close one eye and look inside the tube with the open eye. It is dark inside the tube.

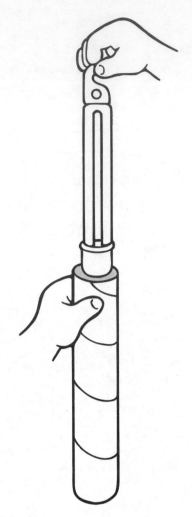

2 Remove the light stick from the package and drop it into the tube. Again, look inside the tube as before. It is still dark inside the tube.

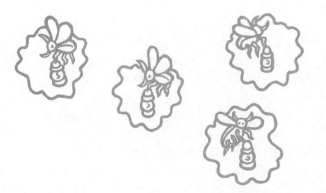

3 Adult Step Remove the light stick from the tube, and activate the light by following the instructions on the package.

4 Again, drop the light stick into the tube and look inside the tube. The light stick gives off light and the inside of the tube glows.

So Now We Know

When the light stick was activated, a glass tube inside it broke and chemicals mixed together. The mixing of the chemicals produced light. A firefly, like the light stick, gives off light when chemicals in its abdomen mix together.

In most kinds of fireflies, the female is wingless or has very short wings. Because of this, the male does most of the flying and the female usually remains on the ground or on low plants. They find each other by flashing their lights. Here's how to make a male firefly model:

- Fold the brown paper in half lengthwise. Cut the paper in half along the fold line.

- Wrap half the paper around the bottle and secure with tape.

- Press the top of the paper around the neck of the bottle and secure with tape. This paper-covered area will be the firefly's thorax.

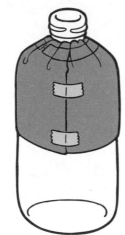

- Screw the lid on the bottle and glue the eyes to the top of the lid.

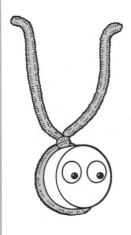

- Wrap the craft stem around the neck of the bottle and bend the ends to form antennae above the eyes.

- Fold the remaining half of the brown paper in half twice, making a 3-by-5-inch (7.5-by-12.5-cm) rectangle.

- Draw the wing and leg patterns on the top layer of the folded paper.

- **Adult Step** Cut out the drawings, cutting through all four layers. Discard one of the leg cutouts.

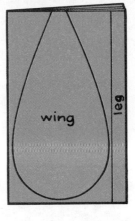

- Arrange the 4 wings in a fanlike pattern with the front wings overlapping the hind wings. Glue them to the upper side of the thorax.

- Glue 3 of the leg cutouts by their centers to the underside of the thorax. Bend the ends, forming 6 legs.

- Unscrew the lid, place the activated light stick inside the bottle, then replace the lid. You now have a model of a male firefly that glows with a cool light.

Eating

Munchers

round up these things

¼-by-6-inch (0.63-by-15-cm) strip of paper
ruler
transparent tape
pliers
hand soap
tap water
paper towel
cookie
mirror

later you'll need

another cookie
glass of milk

1 Bend up 2½ inches (6.25 cm) of each end of the paper strip.

2 Bend out ½ inch (1.25 cm) of each end of the paper strip.

3 Tape the center of the paper strip to the pliers as shown. The pliers represent a bug and the paper strip represents the bug's antennae.

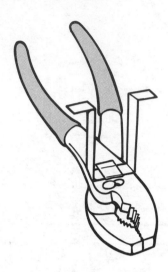

4 Open the jaws of the pliers and use your fingertip to feel the parts that would touch if the jaws were closed. The jaws of the pliers feel rough, like the jaws of some insects.

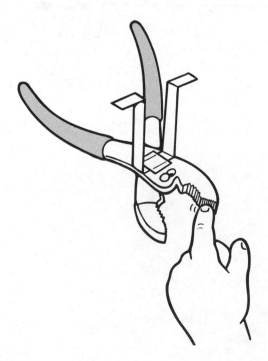

5 Wash and dry your hands.

6 Open your mouth and feel the parts of your back teeth that touch when your mouth is closed. The surfaces of your teeth feel rough.

7 Hold the handles of the pliers, one in each hand, and open and close the jaws as shown. The jaws of the pliers open and close from side to side like the jaws of some insects.

8 Take a bite out of the cookie and eat it. Watch the motion of your jaws in the mirror as you chew. Your lower jaw moves up and down as your teeth crush the cookie.

chomp! chomp!

So Now We Know

Bugs don't have teeth like yours, but some, such as grasshoppers, have rough ridges on their jaws that are used for cutting and chewing food. These jaws open and close sideways, like the pliers, instead of up and down like your jaws.

More Fun Things to Know and Do

Not all insects have "chewing" mouth-parts. Some, such as houseflies, have soaking and sucking mouthparts. The sucking mouthpart is a tube called a proboscis, which has a spongelike tip. A fly soaks up liquids with the spongy tip of its proboscis, then sucks the liquids into its body. Here's how you can eat like a fly:

• Dip the edge of a cookie into a glass of milk.

• Place the wet end of the cookie in your mouth and suck the milk from it.

131

Sippers

I wonder... How do butterflies drink?

Let's find out!

round up these things

3-ounce (90-ml) paper cup
sheet of colored construction paper (any flower color)
pencil
scissors
¼ teaspoon (1.25 ml) sugar
1 tablespoon (15 ml) tap water
spoon
drinking straw

later you'll need

party blower

1 Turn the cup upside down and set it in the center of the paper.

2 With the pencil, trace around the outside of the cup.

3 Remove the cup and draw 6 large flower petals around the circle on the paper. Add a seam line as shown.

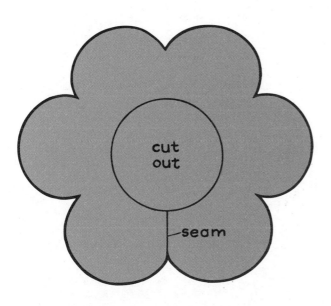

cut out

seam

4 Adult Step Cut out the flower. Cut along the seam line, and then cut out the inner circle of the flower.

5 Slip the paper cup through the hole in the flower.

6 Put the sugar and the water in the cup. Stir.

7 Stand the straw in the cup and sip the water.

So Now We Know

Inside flowers there is a sweet liquid called nectar. A butterfly drinks the nectar in flowers with a proboscis, a long feeding tube. You used a straw to drink the "nectar" in your paper flower.

When a butterfly is not feeding, its proboscis is coiled up. The proboscis uncoils like a party blower when the butterfly wants to drink nectar from inside a flower. Use an upside-down party blower to show how a butterfly's proboscis coils and uncoils.

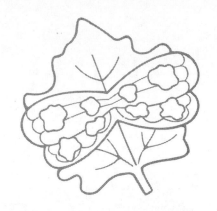

Camouflaging

Hide-and-Seek

Let's find out!

I wonder . . . Why are walkingsticks hard to find?

round up these things

craft stick
5 tablespoons (75 ml) plaster of paris
2 tablespoons (30 ml) tap water
3-ounce (90-ml) paper cup
three 12-inch (30-cm) brown chenille craft
  stems (available at craft stores) or pipe
  cleaners
scissors
ruler

later you'll need

scissors
ruler
20 or more chenille craft stems in different
  colors
100 feet (30 m) of string
friend

1. Use the craft stick to mix the plaster of paris and the water in the paper cup. Discard the craft stick. *NOTE: Do not wash plaster down the drain. It can clog the drain.*

2. Bend one of the craft stems into a V shape. Push the bent end into the wet plaster. This craft stem will be the two main stems of a bush. Allow the plaster to harden before starting the next step. This takes about 2 hours.

3. **Adult Step** Cut the second craft stem into 4 equal parts.

4. Twist the pieces around the stems in the plaster as shown to form branches on the bush.

5. **Adult Step** Cut a 4-inch (10-cm) piece from the third craft stem. Cut the remaining piece into four 2-inch (5-cm) pieces.

6. Twist the 4 shorter craft stem pieces around the longer piece to form 6 legs and 2 antennae as shown. You have made a walkingstick, an insect that looks like a small stick with branches.

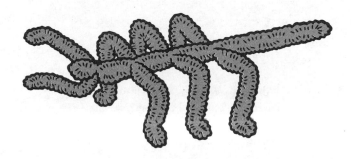

7. Place the walkingstick on the bush. It is hard to tell the walkingstick from the branches.

So Now We Know

The shape and the color of a walkingstick are so much like the twigs of a tree that it is hard to see a walkingstick in a tree. This protects the walkingstick from animals that would eat it.

137

Many insects blend in with their surroundings because they are the same shape and/or color as their surroundings. Here's an insect hide-and-seek game to play:

- Use the craft stems to make 20 or more insects. The insects should have different shapes and be different colors.

- Lay a string on the ground outdoors to mark a continuous trail about 100 feet (30 m) long. The trail should have grass, trees, and flowers, if possible.

- Without anyone watching, place the insects along one side of the string trail. The insects should be hard to see, but still visible.

- Take a friend outdoors and point out the side of the trail where the insects have been placed. Give your friend one minute to walk along the string trail and find as many insects as possible.

- If you have a number of friends who want to search, make more insects, have several trails, and search in teams.

Top and Bottom

I wonder . . .
Why is the top of
a butterfly's wings
a different color
than the bottom?

Let's find
out!

RED
BLUE

scissors
ruler
9-by-12-inch (22.5-by-30-cm) sheet of
  brown construction paper
black marking pen
2 cotton swabs
craft paints, red and
yellow

doll pin (wooden clip clothespin, available
  at craft stores)
two 12-inch (30-cm) black chenille craft
  stems (available at craft stores) or pipe
  cleaners

1 Draw a line across one end of the paper, 4 inches (10 cm) from the end. Cut across the line, keeping the 4-inch (10-cm)-wide strip for the next step. Keep the larger piece of paper for step 10.

2 Fold the strip of paper in half, short ends together.

3 Draw the outline of a pair of butterfly wings on the paper as shown. Make the straight section along the fold about 1 inch (2.5 cm) long.

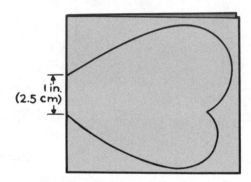

4 **Adult Step**   Cut out the wing drawing, cutting through both layers of paper. Do not cut the wings apart on the fold line.

5 Unfold the wings, then use the pen to draw a curved line between the top and bottom wings as shown. Draw the line on both the front and the back of the wings.

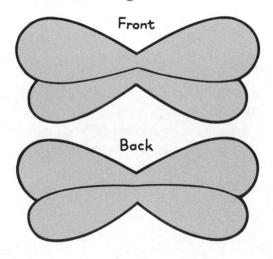

6 On the front of the wings, use the pen to draw a design that is the same on both the right and left wings as shown.

7 Use the swabs to place one blob each of red and yellow paint on one of the top wings and one of the bottom wings as shown. Discard the swabs.

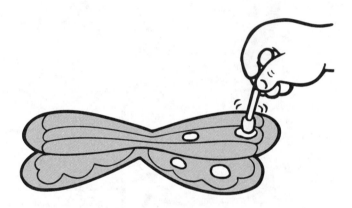

8 While the paint is still wet, refold the wings, painted sides together. Use your fingers to press the paint blobs and spread the wet paint as much as possible.

9 Unfold the wings and allow the paint to dry.

10 On the remaining piece of brown paper, draw a leaf as large as the paper. Cut out the leaf. Use the pen to draw veins in the leaf.

11 Lay the wings, painted side up, on the brown leaf. The colored wings are very easy to see.

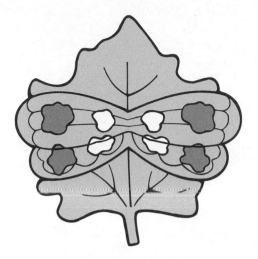

12 Fold the wings so that the colored sides are close together. Stand the folded wings on the leaf. The color of the underside of the wings and the color of the leaf blend together.

So Now We Know

On the top side, a butterfly's wings are very colorful. These colors are seen when the butterfly has its wings spread open as it flies. On the underside, the butterfly's wings are generally a dull color. When the butterfly rests, it holds its wings together, showing the underside. The dull color blends in with things that the butterfly stands on, making it hard to see the butterfly.

More Fun Things to Know and Do

Here's how to make a butterfly using the wings from the original experiment:

- Use the pen to draw 2 large eyes on the rounded end of the doll pin.

- **Adult Step** Cut the 2 craft stems in half.

- Twist the pieces of craft stem around the doll pin to form 6 legs and 2 antennae as shown.

- Fold the wings, colored sides together. Run a bead of glue along both sides of the folded edge.

- Slip the folded edge in the slit of the doll pin. Open the wings.

The colored side of the wings should be face up, with the larger wing pair toward the head.

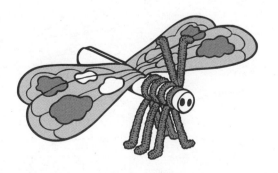

Spinning

Over the Edge

I wonder... Are spiders insects?

Let's find out!

round up these things

lid from a 1-quart (1-liter) jar
4-by-6-inch (10-by-15-cm) piece of
  colored poster board (Red or yellow
  works well.)
pencil
scissors
black pen
one-hole paper punch

two 12-inch (30-cm) black chenille craft
  stems (available at craft stores) or pipe
  cleaners
transparent tape

later you'll need

spider made in original experiment
12 inches (30 cm) of sewing thread
transparent tape

1 Lay the lid near one end of the poster board.

2 Use the pencil to trace around the lid.

3 Move the lid up so that it slightly overlaps the first tracing, then again trace around the lid.

4 Draw part of a circle at the top of the second circle, following the picture shown. You have drawn the outline of a spider. Mark UNDERSIDE on the spider as shown.

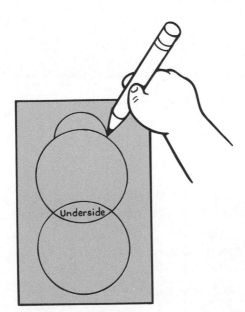

5 **Adult Step** Cut around the outside lines of the spider.

6 Turn the spider over and use the pen to draw eight eyes on its head and a curved line between the two body parts. The spider has two body parts. The part with eyes is called the cephalothorax and the other part is called the abdomen.

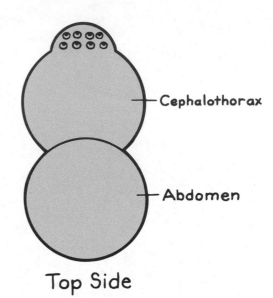

Top Side

7 Use the paper punch to make four holes on each side of the cephalo-thorax, as shown in the picture.

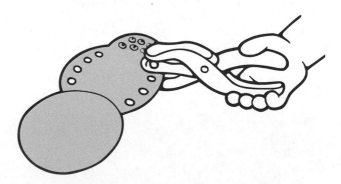

8 **Adult Step** Cut the craft stems in half and stick them through the holes as shown. Adjust the stems so the spider's eight legs are the same length.

9 On the underside, place a piece of tape across the stems to hold them in place.

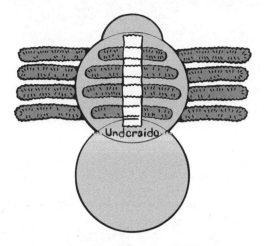

10 Bend the stems to form eight legs. Keep the spider for the next experiment.

So Now We Know

You can tell from the number of body parts and legs that spiders are not insects. Insects have three main body parts and six legs. Spiders have two main body parts and eight legs.

More Fun Things to Know and Do

Spiders make silk threads. These threads come from holes on the underside of the spider's abdomen. Most spiders have a cord of silk called a dragline trailing behind them. Spiders can use the dragline to gently drop to the ground or turn around and climb back up. Here's how you can show that a dragline protects a spider:

- Take the spider from the original experiment and tape one end of the thread to one end of the underside of the spider's abdomen. The thread is your spider's dragline.

- Tape the free end of the dragline to the edge of a table.

- Move the spider around on the table, then push it off the edge. The dragline keeps the spider from falling to the

floor. A real spider could climb up its dragline and get back on the table.

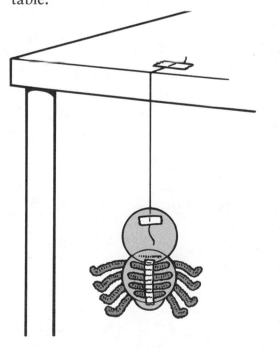

Spiderlings

round up these things

coffee can lid
file folder
pencil
scissors
ruler
pen
paper fastener

later you'll need

scissors
ruler
sewing thread
typing paper
school glue

146

1 Lay the coffee can lid on the file folder.

2 Use the pencil to trace around the lid.

3 **Adult Step**   Cut out the circle, cutting through both layers of the file folder.

4 Use the ruler and the pencil to draw two lines on each of the paper circles. The lines must cross and divide the circles into four equal parts.

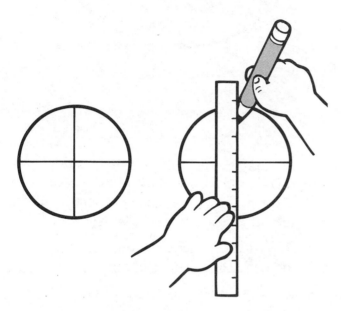

5 **Adult Step** On one of the paper circles, cut away part of one of the four sections as shown.

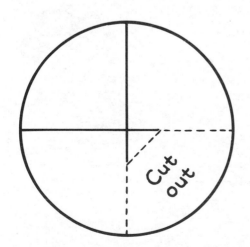

6 Turn the paper circle over and print the word SPIDER on the plain side.

7 On the second paper circle, use the pencil to draw and label the four steps of how a spider grows as shown. Use the pen to trace over your drawings and labels.

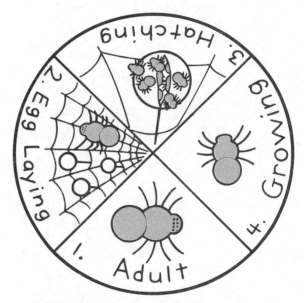

8 **Adult Step**   Use the pencil to make a hole through the center of each paper circle.

9 Place the circles together, one on top of the other, so that the cutout opening is on top with the word SPIDER showing. The pictures on the bottom circle should show through the cutout.

10 Secure the circles together with the paper fastener. This will be your spider growth wheel.

11 Lay the wheel on a table, and then hold the top circle with one hand and turn the bottom circle counterclockwise with the other hand. The four steps are seen in the cutout as the bottom circle turns.

So Now We Know

Spiders come from eggs. They hatch as little spiderlings and grow into adults.

More Fun Things to Know and Do

There are many little spiderlings in most egg sacs. After hatching, a spiderling climbs onto branches, outdoor tables, and other surfaces; then it releases strands of silk. These silk strands and the attached spiderling are lifted by the wind and float to a new area. This is called ballooning and most spiders do this. Here's a way to show ballooning by spiderlings:

- **Adult Step** Cut 3 pieces of thread, each about 6 inches (15 cm) long.

- Tear a penny-size piece from the typing paper.

- Coat the piece of paper with glue.

- Place one end of each thread on the sticky side of the paper.

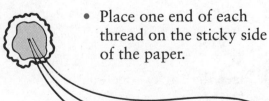

- Fold the paper, with the sticky sides together, over the glued ends of the threads. The paper is a spiderling and the threads are its strands of silk.

- Repeat this procedure four times to make five spiderlings in all.

- Lay the spiderlings together on a table.

- Lean toward the table so that your mouth is close to but not touching the spiderlings. Then, blow as hard as you can. Where did your spiderlings land?

Let's find out!

Part Four | # THE HUMAN BODY

Skin

Pleated

round up these things

flexible drinking straw

later you'll need

water-soluble black felt-tip pen

1 Try to bend the straw where it is not wrinkled. It is difficult to bend.

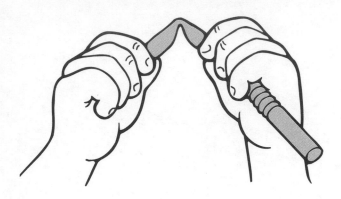

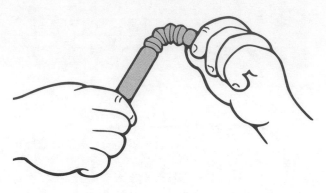

So Now We Know

The skin at your elbows has large wrinkles like the straw. These wrinkles let you bend your arm easily. The skin at other places in your body that bend, such as your knees, toes, and fingers, also has large wrinkles.

2 Try to bend the straw where it is wrinkled. The wrinkles stretch out and the straw bends easily.

More Fun Things to Know and Do

Look at the skin around the parts of your body that bend, such as your knees, toes, and fingers. Here's a way to show off some wrinkles:

- With the felt-tip pen, draw a caterpillar on the underside of your finger as shown.

- Bend and stretch your finger. When you bend your finger, part of the caterpillar disappears in the wrinkled skin. When you stretch your finger, the skin smooths out and all of the caterpillar can be seen.

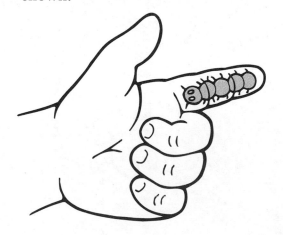

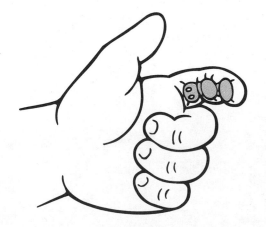

Puckered

round up these things

new cellulose kitchen sponge
bowl of tap water
scissors
ruler
petroleum jelly

later you'll need

bowl of tap water
timer

1 Rinse the sponge in the bowl of water and squeeze out as much water as possible.

2 **Adult Step** Cut a 1-inch (2.5cm)-wide strip from the sponge. Keep the strip.

3 **Adult Step** Cut a section from the sponge strip so that about half of the sponge is half as thick.

4 Allow the sponge strip to dry thoroughly. This may take several hours.

5 Press on the dry sponge strip with your fingers, making it as flat as possible.

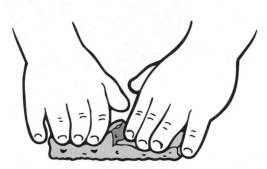

6 Thoroughly cover the surface of the thinner section of the sponge strip with petroleum jelly.

7 Dip your pointer finger into the water in the bowl and hold your wet finger above the part of the sponge coated with petroleum jelly. Allow 2 to 3 water drops to fall onto the sponge. The water drops form round balls that sit on top of the sponge.

8 Dip your finger again into the water and allow 2 to 3 water drops to fall onto the uncoated part of the sponge. The sponge puckers up where the water falls.

So Now We Know

The skin on the tips of your fingers and toes is different than the rest of your skin. It is thicker, and like the uncoated part of the sponge it is not waterproofed with a coating of oil. That's why it soaks up water and puckers up when you have been in water for a long time.

More Fun Things to Know and Do

Lets see how the rest of your skin keeps out water:

- Dip your finger in the water in the bowl.

- Hold your wet finger above the back of your other hand. Let 2 to 3 drops of water fall onto your hand.

- Observe the water on your skin for 5 to 10 seconds or longer. The water drops sit on your skin and do not sink in.

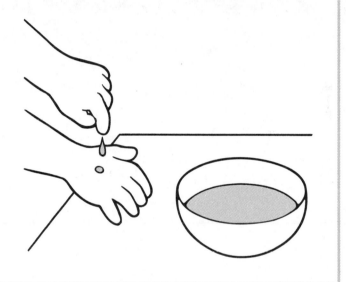

Hair

Hairy

I wonder . . . Why do I have hair on my body?

Let's find out!

round up these things	later you'll need
box, at least 2 inches (5 cm) taller and wider than a 1-quart (1-liter) jar cotton balls two 1-quart (1-liter) jars with lids 2-cup (500-ml) measuring cup tap water 2 bulb-type thermometers timer	newspaper art paintbrush with hair bristles container of powder, such as baby powder ruler

1 Cover the bottom of the box with a layer of cotton balls.

2 Set one jar in the box. Leave the other jar on the table.

3 Fill the box with cotton balls up to the top of the jar.

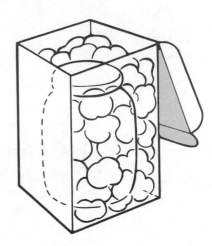

4 **Adult Step**   Use the measuring cup to add 2 cups (500 ml) of hot tap water to each jar.

5 Stand a thermometer in each jar of hot water.

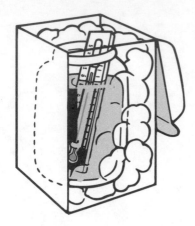

6 After 1 minute, remove the thermometers and compare the height of the liquid in each. The heights are the same or nearly the same.

7 Seal each jar with a lid.

8 Quickly cover the jar in the box with a layer of cotton balls and close the lid on the box.

9 Set the timer for 10 minutes.

10 At the end of 10 minutes, uncover the jars and stand a thermometer in each jar.

11 After 1 minute, remove the thermometers and again compare the height of the liquid in each thermometer.

> The thermometer's liquid in the jar surrounded by the cotton balls is higher. This means the water in this jar is warmer.

So Now We Know

Hair on your body helps to keep heat from leaving your body the same way the cotton balls helped to keep heat from leaving the water.

More Fun Things to Know and Do

You have hair in your nose and ears. There is also hair above your eyes, called eyebrows, and on your eyelids, called eyelashes. Small dust and dirt specks stick to these hairs and help keep the specks from entering your nose, ears, and eyes. Here's a way to see how things stick to hair:

- Spread the newspaper on a table.

- Look at the bristles on the art brush. They should be clean.

- Hold the art brush above the newspaper.

- Ask your helper to hold the container of powder so that its open end is about 12 inches (30 cm) from the art brush. Then, spray the powder toward the brush by squeezing the container.

- Again look at the bristles on the brush. Powder sticks to the hairs on the brush.

Curly

round up these things

scissors
ruler
sheet of typing paper

later you'll need

straw in a paper wrapper
cup
tap water

1 Cut a 1-by-6-inch (2.5-by-15-cm) strip of paper.

2 Hold the ends of the paper in your hands.

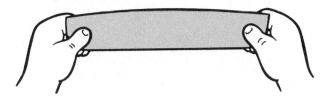

3 Place the strip of paper on the table with one end over the edge.

4 Press the paper tightly against the edge of the table. Keeping the paper taut, pull down on the paper, sliding the entire strip across the table edge.

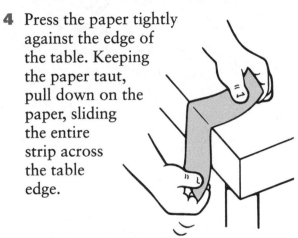

5 Hold one end of the paper. The paper curls up.

So Now We Know

Strands of curly hair bend around. Rubbing the paper in the experiment bent the paper, so it curled up.

More Fun Things to Know and Do

Moist air can make hair twist and bend. Here's a way to see how water changes the shape of hair:

- Stand the paper-wrapped straw on a table and push the paper wrapper down around the straw until the wrapper is as squashed as possible.

- Take the squashed wrapper off the straw and put it on the table.

- Fill the cup half full with water.

- Dip your finger in the water. Use your finger to put 1 drop of water on a section of the wrapper. Dip your finger in the water again and put a drop of water on another section of the wrapper.

- Watch the wrapper twist and bend.

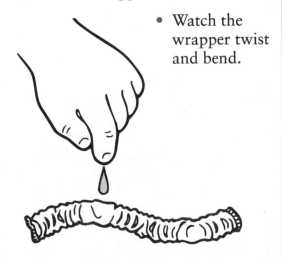

Skeleton

Movable

round up these things

6 thread spools
4-by-5-inch (10-by-12.5-cm) poster board
pencil
scissors
one-hole paper punch
12-inch (30-cm) piece of string
transparent tape
ruler

later you'll need

sheet of typing paper
masking tape
book
pencil

1 Place the flat end of a thread spool on the poster board.

2 Draw five circles on the poster board by tracing around the end of the spool.

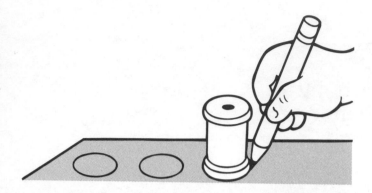

3 Cut out the five circles and use the paper punch to make a hole in the center of each circle.

4 Thread one end of the string through the hole in one of the spools, then tape the end of the string to the end of the spool.

5 Stand the spool on end and thread the free end of the string through the hole in one of the poster board circles. Continue to add spools and circles to the string until all are used. Then, tape the end of the string to the top spool.

6 Holding the bottom spool on a table, push the top spool about 2 inches (5 cm) to one side.

7 Push the spool in different directions.

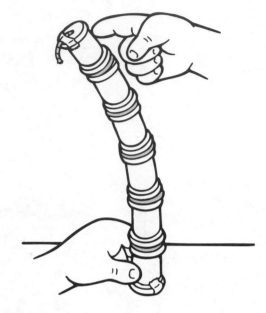

So Now We Know

Your backbone is made of separate bones called vertebrae. When you bend, your vertebrae, like the spools, separate a little so your back can move. Each vertebra has a hole through its back part through which the spinal cord is threaded. Between each vertebra is a pad, like the circle, called a disk. Disks keep the vertebrae from rubbing against each other.

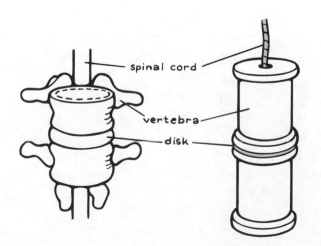

You are taller in the morning than you are at night. This is because your vertebrae separate during the night when you are lying down, but gravity pulls them together during the day when you stand or sit up. Here's a way to see how much your height changes from morning to evening:

- On the day before the experiment, hold a sheet of paper to the wall so that the top of your head is about even with the middle of the paper.

- Tape the paper to the wall.

- The next morning, as soon as you wake up, measure your height by standing against the wall with your head against the paper. Stand as straight as possible.

- Ask your helper to place a book on your head as in the diagram.

- Ask your helper to make a mark on the paper where the bottom of

the book touches the paper. Write MORNING next to the mark.

- In the evening of that same day, measure your height again. Write EVENING next to the mark.

- Compare the morning and evening marks. The morning mark will be a little higher than the evening mark.

Rubbery

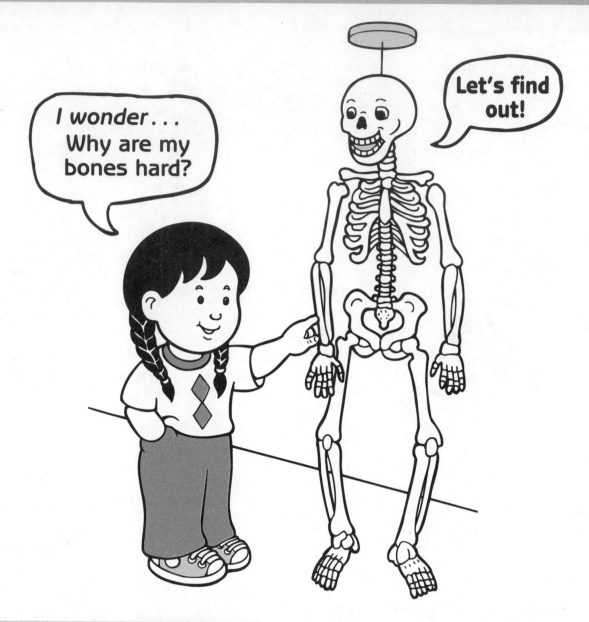

knife (to be used only by an adult)
cooked chicken leg
dishwashing liquid
1-quart (1-liter) jar with lid
3 cups (750 ml) white vinegar
tongs
NOTE: *Wash your hands each time after handling the chicken bone.*

sheet of typing paper
transparent tape
this book

1 **Adult Step** Cut as much of the meat off the bone as possible.

2 Wash the bone in soapy water and rinse.

3 Try to bend the leg bone with your fingers.

4 Place the bone in the jar.

5 Add the vinegar to the jar.

6 Secure the lid on the jar.

7 After 24 hours, remove the lid. Use the tongs to remove the bone from the jar.

8 Rinse the vinegar off the bone with water.

9 Try bending the bone again.

10 Replace the bone in the jar of vinegar and secure the lid.

11 Repeat steps 7 through 10 each day for 7 or more days. The bone will gradually become easier to bend.

So Now We Know

Bones are hard because they contain a chemical called calcium. The vinegar removes the calcium in the bone, making the bone rubbery. If you didn't have calcium in your bones, you wouldn't be able to stand or move your body.

The long bone in your leg, called your thigh bone, is shaped much like the chicken leg bone. Both have a hollow, cylinderlike shape, which means they're shaped like a tall soup can. Here's a way to make a model of your thigh bone to see how its shape makes it strong:

- Roll the paper into a tube, overlapping the top and bottom edges.

- Tape the ends together as shown.

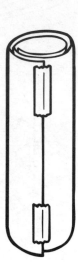

- Stand the tube on a table and lay this book on top of the tube. The paper tube is strong enough to support the weight of the book.

Circulation

Plugged

round up these things

jar, ½ pint (250 ml) or smaller (the smaller
  the mouth, the better)
tap water
scissors
cheesecloth
rubber band
large bowl

later you'll need

3 to 4 purple grapes
paper towel
resealable plastic bag

1 Fill the jar about half full with water.

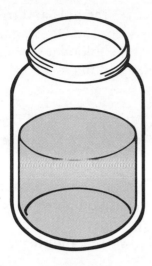

2 Cut three squares from the cheese-cloth large enough to cover the mouth of the jar.

3 Lay the cloth squares one at a time across the mouth of the jar. Position the cloth squares so that the threads crisscross, forming small openings between them.

4 Put the rubber band over the cloth and around the neck of the jar so that the rubber band holds the cloth squares securely against the jar.

5 Set the bowl on a table.

6 Hold the jar upright over the bowl, then quickly turn the jar upside down. At first, some of the water will pour out of the jar, but most of it will stay inside.

So Now We Know

Water fills the holes between the over-lapped threads and stops the water from flowing out of the jar. When you cut yourself, tiny, sticky, threadlike materials in the blood cover the hole and trap the blood. This stops the bleeding. At the surface, the trapped blood and the threadlike materials dry and make a hard scab.

More Fun Things to Know and Do

When you hit yourself on something hard, you may develop a bruise. A bruise shows up because the skin is not broken, but blood vessels underneath the skin are. The blood leaks out under the skin. Here's how to make a model showing the formation of a bruise:

- Wrap the grapes in the paper towel.

- Place the towel inside the plastic bag.

- Lay the bag on a table and hit the bag with your hand so that the grapes break. The juice will spread through the fibers of the paper towel without leaking out of the bag. Think of the plastic bag as your skin, the towel as your body under your skin, the grape as a blood vessel, and the grape juice as blood.

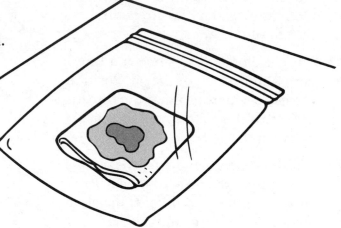

Lub-Dub

cardboard tube from paper towel roll

cardboard tube
watch

1 In a quiet room, ask your helper to hold the paper tube against the center of his or her chest.

2 Place one of your ears over the other end of the tube.

3 Stand very still and listen to the sound of your helper's heart.

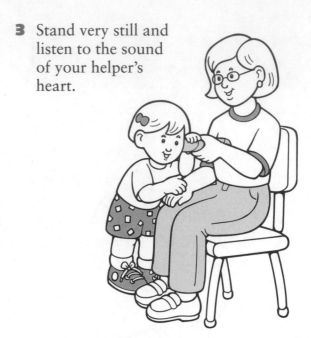

So Now We Know

Your helper's heart made a "lub-dub" sound. Your doctor uses a stethoscope to listen to people's hearts. Your paper tube acts like a stethoscope to make the heart-beat sound louder.

More Fun Things to Know and Do

Each time your heart beats, it pumps blood through your body. Blood carries nutrients and oxygen to all parts of your body. Nutrients come from the food you eat and oxygen comes from the air you breathe. When you exercise, your body needs more nutrients and oxygen. This means your heart has to pump faster. Here's a way to find out how a heart sounds after exercising:

- Ask your helper to run in place for 1 minute.

- Use your paper stethoscope to listen to your helper's heart. Does it sound louder and faster? Softer and slower?

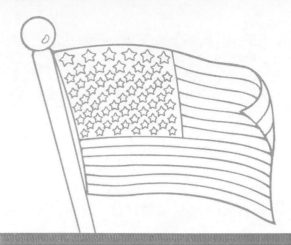

Respiration

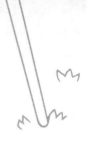

In and Out

I wonder...
Why does my chest move when I breathe?

Let's find out!

round up these things

paper lunch bag

later you'll need

scissors
2-liter soda bottle
9-inch (22.5-cm) round balloon
ruler
plastic trash bag
rubber band
Band-Aid

1 Lie on your back.

2 Hold the paper bag over your mouth with one hand and place the other hand on your chest.

3 Breathe deeply several times. As you breathe, watch the bag and feel your chest. When you breath in, the bag will empty and your chest will go up.

When you breathe out, the bag will fill up and your chest will go down.

So Now We Know

You have two air bags in your chest called lungs that fill with air when you breathe in. When you breathe out, air moves out of your lungs.

Your chest is like a room with a muscle for a floor. This muscle is called the diaphragm. Your lungs fill most of the space in this room. When the diaphragm moves up, the room gets smaller and air is forced out of your lungs. When the diaphragm moves down, the room is larger and air rushes into your lungs. Here's a way to show how the diaphragm works to fill your lungs:

- **Adult Step** Cut off and discard the bottom of the soda bottle.

- Put the balloon inside the bottle, stretching the mouth of the balloon over the mouth of the bottle. The balloon represents a lung.

- **Adult Step** Cut a circle with a 10-inch (25-cm) diameter from the plastic bag.

- Turn the bottle upside down.

- **Adult Step** Lay the plastic circle over the cutaway end of the bottle, draw the edges of the plastic around the bottle, and secure the

plastic with the rubber band. The plastic represents a diaphragm.

- Stick the ends of the Band-Aid to the middle of the plastic so that it makes a pull tab.

- Hold the bottle upright with one hand and pull the Band-Aid down slightly with the other hand. Notice how the balloon fills up when the plastic diaphragm is pulled down.

- Push the plastic up and watch the balloon deflate.

Frosty

round up these things	later you'll need
ice cube	drinking straw
resealable plastic sandwich bag	1-gallon (4-liter) resealable plastic bag
hand mirror	sheet of black construction paper
	desk lamp or window with direct light
	magnifying lens

1 Place the ice cube in the plastic bag and seal the bag.

2 Lay the plastic bag on the mirror.

3 Gently press the ice against the mirror and rub it back and forth over the mirror's surface several times to cool the glass.

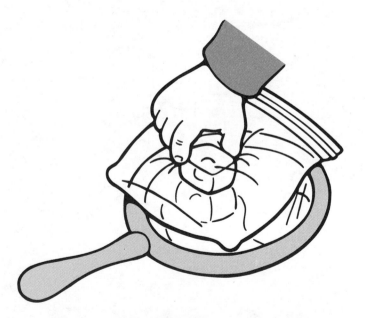

4 Remove the bag of ice and immediately hold the mirror close to, but not touching, your mouth. Exhale on the mirror. The mirror looks foggy.

So Now We Know

Your breath has water in it that you can't see. When you breathe into cold air or on the cold mirror, the water in your breath collects into a cloud of tiny drops of water that you can see.

You exhale water into the air with each breath you take. Here's another way to see the water you exhale:

• Place the end of the straw in the plastic bag and seal the bag up to the straw.

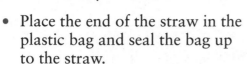

• Take a deep breath, exhale through the straw, and then immediately remove the straw from the bag and press the opening of the bag shut.

• Lay the paper on a table near a lamp or window with direct light.

• Place the bag on top of the paper. The inside of the bag is fogged with water from your exhaled breath.

• Look at the bag with the magnifying lens. Different-size water drops can be seen on the inside of the bag.

Digestion

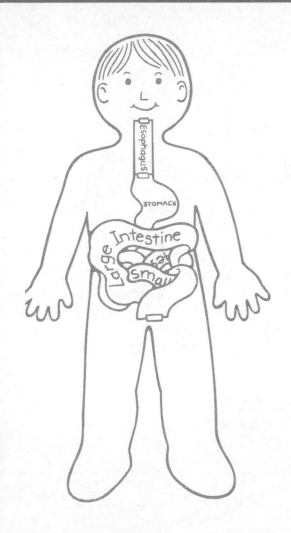

Choppers

apple

scissors
brown construction paper
small empty box, such as for rice
transparent tape
1-inch (2.5-cm)-wide roll of masking tape
serrated knife (to be used only by an adult)
marker
crayons

1 Take a bite from the apple using your front teeth.

2 First, try to chew the bite from the apple with your front teeth.

3 Then, chew the piece of apple in your mouth with your back teeth and swallow it.

4 Try to bite the apple with the teeth on the side of your mouth.

5 Chew any piece of apple in your mouth and swallow it.

So Now We Know

Your front teeth are wide and thin at the edges. They are best at biting food and not very good at chewing. The teeth in the back of your mouth have large, uneven top surfaces. These teeth are best at grinding food and not very good at biting.

More Fun Things to Know and Do

Babies are usually born without teeth. By the age of 2, a child usually has 20 teeth, called "milk" teeth or "baby" teeth. Around 6 years of age, the milk teeth begin to be pushed out and replaced by permanent teeth. There are 32 teeth in a full set of adult permanent teeth. Here's how to make a model of milk teeth:

- Cut the paper to fit around the sides of the box.

- Wrap the paper around the sides of the box and secure it with transparent tape.

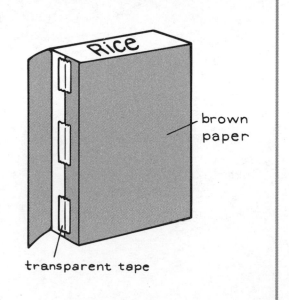

brown paper

transparent tape

- Draw a line around the middle of the box.

- Wrap a strip of masking tape around the box with one edge of the tape along the line drawn around the box. On the opposite side of the line, wrap a second strip of masking tape around the box.

- **Adult Step** Use the knife to cut across the box between the strips of masking tape, but stop at one of the narrow sides of the box as shown.

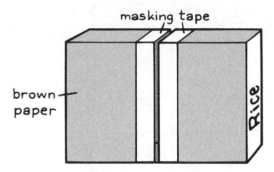

- Use the marker to draw 10 teeth on each strip of masking tape. Follow the picture to see which kind of teeth and how many to draw where.

- With the scissors, cut out the uneven edges of the molars and the pointed tips of the canine teeth.

- Use the crayons to draw a face on the box for fun. Open and close the bottom of the box to make the model chew.

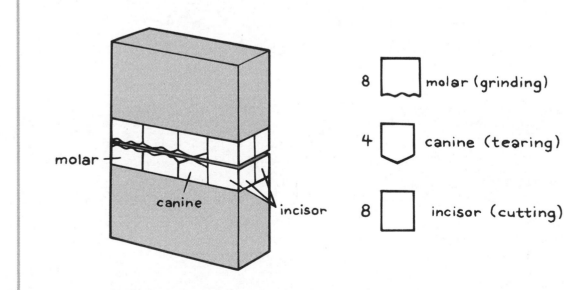

8 molar (grinding)

4 canine (tearing)

8 incisor (cutting)

Tube Chute

I wonder . . . Where does the food I eat go?

Let's find out!

round up these things

ruler
scissors
adding-machine tape
pen
6-inch (15-cm)-square piece of white
  construction paper
two 9-by-12-inch (22.5-by-30-cm) sheets
  of pink construction paper
masking tape

later you'll need

brown butcher or bulletin board paper
  (found at craft or teaching supply stores)
scissors
colored markers or crayons

1 Measure and cut two strips of adding-machine tape. Make one 8 inches (20 cm) long and the other 15 feet (4.5 m) long.

2 Label the short paper strip ESOPHAGUS and the long one SMALL INTESTINE.

3 Use the pen to draw a stomach and label it STOMACH on the white piece of construction paper. Follow the picture to see the size and general shape of the stomach. Make widths A and B on the picture equal to the width of the adding-machine tape.

4 Cut out the drawing of the stomach.

5 Cut the 2 sheets of pink construction paper in half lengthwise. Make a long strip that is 4½ inches (11.25 cm) wide by overlapping the short ends of the 4 pieces of paper about ½ inch (1.25 cm) and connecting them with tape. Label this strip LARGE INTESTINE.

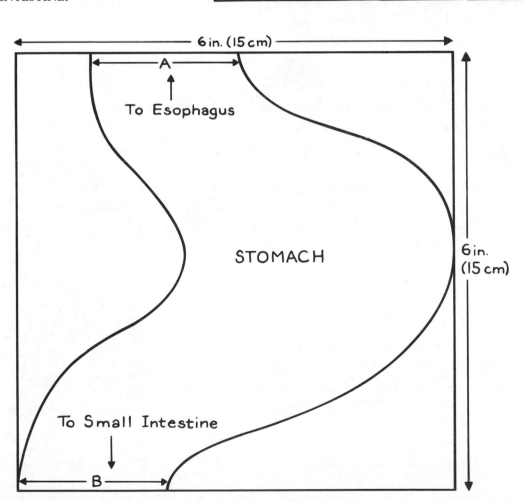

6 Tape the pieces of your model together in this order: esophagus, stomach, small intestine, and large intestine. Stretch the paper sheets out as straight as possible on the floor.

So Now We Know

You have made a model of your digestive tubes. These tubes are the path that the food you swallow takes through your body.

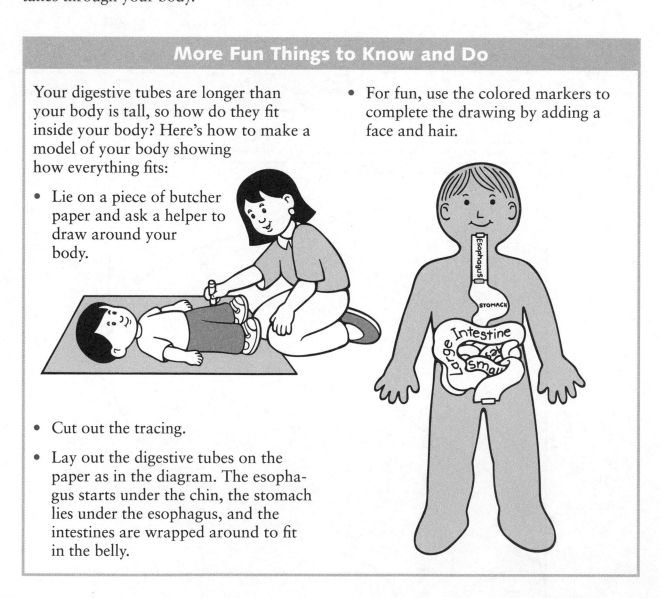

More Fun Things to Know and Do

Your digestive tubes are longer than your body is tall, so how do they fit inside your body? Here's how to make a model of your body showing how everything fits:

- Lie on a piece of butcher paper and ask a helper to draw around your body.

- Cut out the tracing.

- Lay out the digestive tubes on the paper as in the diagram. The esophagus starts under the chin, the stomach lies under the esophagus, and the intestines are wrapped around to fit in the belly.

- For fun, use the colored markers to complete the drawing by adding a face and hair.

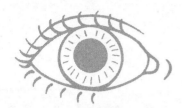

Senses

Big and Little

I wonder . . .
Why do my eyes look red in some photos?

Let's find out!

cereal bowl
sheet of typing paper
pencil
drinking glass
crayons
dime
scissors
aluminum foil

rubber band
flashlight
ruler
quarter

hand mirror
watch

1 Place the bowl upside down in the center of the paper.

2 Use the pencil to draw around the outside of the bowl.

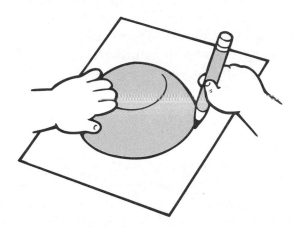

3 Turn the glass upside down in the center of the circle and draw around the outside of the glass.

4 Use a crayon to color the inside circle the same color as your eyes.

5 Lay the dime in the center of the colored circle and draw around it with the pencil.

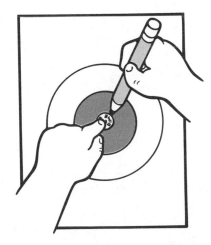

6 **Adult Step** Cut out the small circle in the center of the paper. The hole represents the black dot in your eye, called the pupil.

7 Line the bowl with aluminum foil.

8 Place the paper over the foil-lined bowl so that the hole in the paper is over the center of the bowl.

9 Secure the paper with the rubber band.

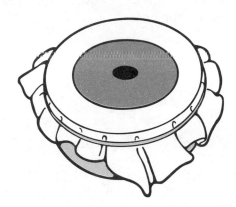

10 Set the bowl on a table and hold the flashlight about 6 inches (15 cm) above the hole in the paper. The light from the flashlight enters the hole in the paper, bounces off the aluminum foil that lines the bowl, and shines back out the hole. Look at the hole and notice how bright it looks.

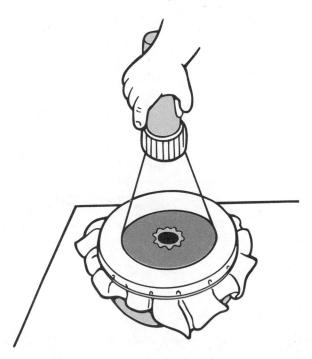

11 Take the paper off the bowl, lay the quarter in the center over the hole, and draw around the quarter.

12 Adult Step Cut out the circle on the paper.

13 Repeat steps 8 through 10. Notice that more light bounces out through the larger hole.

So Now We Know

The pupils in your eyes are really holes covered with see-through skin. When you are photographed, the light from the camera's flash enters the eye through your pupil. Some of the light bounces back toward the camera. Your eyes look red in a photo when your pupils are very large. More light is going into your eyes, and more of the light bounces off the red blood vessels in the back of your eye.

More Fun Things to Know and Do

Your pupils get smaller in bright light and larger in the dark. Here's a way to see how light changes the size of your pupils:

- Sit in a brightly lit room or outside in the sunshine. CAUTION: *Never look directly at the sun because it can permanently damage your eyes.*

- Close one eye and leave the other eye open.

- Cup one hand over the closed eye. Hold a mirror in the other hand.

- Look at the pupil of the open eye in the mirror.

- After 2 to 3 minutes, open the closed eye and quickly look at its pupil in the mirror.

Tasty

round up these things

½ teaspoon (2.5 ml) sugar
½ teaspoon (2.5 ml) salt
½ teaspoon (2.5 ml) unsweetened cocoa
   powder
½ teaspoon (2.5 ml) lemonade powder
plate
drinking glass
tap water
4 cotton swabs

later you'll need

3 different kinds of fruit juice
four 3-ounce (90 ml) paper cups
tap water
scarf that can be used as a blindfold

1 Place the sugar, salt, cocoa, and lemonade in separate areas on the plate.

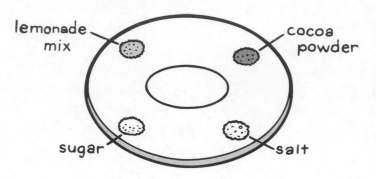

lemonade mix

cocoa powder

sugar

salt

2 Fill the glass with water.

3 Dip a cotton swab in the water, touch it to the sugar in the plate, and then lick the swab with your tongue. Discard the swab.

4 Swallow the food and decide if the food tasted sweet, salty, bitter, or sour.

5 Drink some water to wash out the taste of the food.

6 Repeat steps 3 and 4, using the other three foods.

So Now We Know

Your tongue has bumps on it called taste buds. These let your tongue taste things that are sweet, salty, bitter, and sour. The sugar is sweet, the salt is salty, the cocoa is bitter, and the lemonade is sour.

The taste of food depends not only on your tongue but also on your nose. Here's a way to discover that certain tastes are a combination of flavor and smell:

- So that the tester does not know what juice is being tested, prepare the drinks before the experiment. Pour each fruit juice into a cup. Fill the fourth cup with water.

- Blindfold the tester so that the drinks cannot be identified by sight.

- Instruct the tester to pinch his or her nose closed during the entire experiment. It is important not to sneak a smell during the experiment.

- Hand one cup of juice to the tester and give instructions to drink the juice and identify it.

- After making the identification, have the tester drink some water to wash out the taste of the juice. Repeat the testing procedure for the other two juices.

water

- Repeat the testing procedure without the tester holding his or her nose.

APPENDIX A
Section Summaries

SCIENCE

Air

Air is a mixture of gases, mainly nitrogen and oxygen. The layer of air surrounding the earth is called the **atmosphere**. Air is invisible. Even though it cannot be seen, we know that air exists by the way it affects other things. For example, a cup or a plastic bag may look empty, but each is actually filled with air. The experiment "Spacey" (page 5) demonstrates that air takes up space.

Air also pushes against falling objects. Things fall because of gravity. **Gravity** is a force that pulls everything toward the center of the earth. (Forces are explored in a later section.) Gravity pulls a parachute down, while air pushes against it and slows its fall. The **canopy** is the part of the parachute that catches the air. A canopy can be round like an umbrella or more rectangular like an airplane wing. The experiment "Drifter" (page 8) demonstrates that air slows falling objects, especially those with a large surface, such as parachutes.

Changes

Much of science is the study of changes. Changes are constantly happening all around us. A change in which a material stays the same is called a **physical change**.

Balls bounce because of a physical change called **elasticity** (the ability of a material to return to its original shape after being pushed or pulled out of shape). Elastic materials are said to be **flexible**. The more flexible the material from which a ball is made, the more bounce the ball has. So, the more quickly a ball recovers its shape, the higher it can bounce. In the experiment "Bouncy Blubber" (page 12), children make a soft rubbery material to demonstrate elasticity.

Another type of change is a chemical change. In a **chemical change**, materials do not stay the same but change into something else. The experiment "Play Clay" (page 15) is a recipe for a chemical change. One clue that a chemical change has occurred in this experiment is that the play clay does not feel or look like the original materials.

Magnets

Only some metals are magnetic. Materials that are not magnetic, such as paper and plastics, allow the **magnetic field** (the area around a magnet in which its magnetic forces can be detected) to pass through the material without any disruptions. This is why a paper can be held between a magnet and a refrigerator door. The experiment "Stickers" (page 19) shows some fun things children can do with magnets to understand the power of magnetic fields.

Near the northernmost point of the earth is a place called the earth's **magnetic north pole**. If a magnet is allowed to swing freely, one pole, or end, will always point toward the earth's magnetic north pole. This end of the magnet is called the **north pole of a magnet**. A **compass** is an instrument used to determine direction by means of a free-swinging magnetic needle. The experiment "North Seekers" (page 22) demonstrates how magnets make a compass work.

Forces

A **force** is a push or a pull in a given direction.

The upward push on an object in a fluid, such as water, is called **buoyancy**. Objects in water sink when their weight is greater than the buoyancy exerted on them by the water. Another factor that determines whether objects sink or float is their density. **Density** is a comparison of **weight** (a force caused by gravity) and size. If two objects weigh the same but are different sizes, the larger object is less dense and more likely to float than the other object is. Buoyancy increases with the weight of the water. Seawater weighs more than freshwater because of the salt in it, so objects float better in the ocean than in freshwater. In the experiment "Floater" (page 26), children explore buoyancy by molding clay into two different shapes, a ball that sinks and a boat that floats. The difference in the shape of the clay changes its size, and, thus, affects its buoyancy.

Things that are moving will continue to move unless some force stops them. This resistance to change in motion is called **inertia**. Without a seat belt, a person in a car continues to move forward when the car suddenly stops. The seat belt pushes against the person and forces the person to stop with the car. In the experiment "Buckle Up" (page 29), children use models to see what happens when a car suddenly stops and the person in the car isn't wearing a seat belt.

Light

A **shadow** is the dark area cast upon a surface by an object that blocks light. When light cannot pass through a material, a shadow is cast. The length of the shadow depends on where the light is. Shadows made by the sun get shorter as the sun rises higher in the sky. When the sun is at its highest point in the sky, little or no shadow is produced. The experiment "Changing" (page 33) shows how shadows change size depending on the position of the light that makes them.

A **rainbow** is an arc-shaped band of colors in the sky. To see a rainbow, there must be water drops in the air and the sun must be behind the viewer. If the sun is higher than 42 degrees above the horizon, no rainbow will appear. Rainbows are produced when white light passes through water in the air and separates into colors. The experiment "Rainbows" (page 36) lets children use water to make rainbows in air and on paper.

Sound

Sounds are made when things **vibrate** (shake or move back and forth repeatedly). The rate at which an object vibrates affects the **pitch** (high or low quality) of the sound produced. As the vibration rate decreases, the pitch gets lower.

A regular telephone works not because the telephone wires vibrate, but because the vibrations of voice sounds are changed into electric signals. The signals travel along wires from the mouthpiece of one telephone to the earpiece of another telephone, where the signals are changed back into sound. In the experiment "String Telephone" (page 39), children make telephones that use cups as both the mouthpiece and the earpiece. The vibrations of the speaker's voice make one cup vibrate. These vibrations travel along the string to the other cup, which vibrates and the speaker's voice is heard.

When a person chews, the teeth hit against each other and against the food in the person's mouth. This causes the teeth to vibrate. The bones in the head pass these vibrations along to the ears. The experiment "Musical Teeth" (page 42) demonstrates that sound waves traveling through solids are louder than sound waves traveling through air.

Electricity

All **matter** (anything that takes up space and has weight) is made up of **atoms** (tiny particles from which all things are made). Atoms are made of positive electric charges called **protons** and negative electric charges called **electrons**. There are an equal number of protons and electrons in each atom. A comb pulled through hair will rub some of the electrons off the hair, leaving the hair with more protons than electrons. The hair is then positively charged, and the comb is negatively charged. The different charges on the comb and the hair cause the comb and the hair to be attracted to each other. This buildup of stationary electric charges in one place is called **static electricity**. In the experiment "Attractive" (page 46), children use static electricity to make a balloon stick to their hair, paper, and a wall.

A **battery** is a device that uses chemicals to produce **current electricity** (a form of energy associated with the movement of electric charges). A flashlight bulb glows when electricity flows through an **electric circuit** (the path that electricity follows), which includes the battery, a foil strip, and a fine wire filament inside the flashlight bulb. When the electricity reaches the wire filament, the wire becomes hot and glows. In the experiment "Flashlight" (page 49), children take apart a flashlight to see how it works.

NATURE

Basic Life-forms

Animals, like all living things, are made of building blocks called **cells**. Most cells are very small and flexible. But bone cells have calcium substances between them that give bones their hardness. Some animal cells are so small that a line of 40,000 of these cells would be about 1 inch (2.5 cm) long. In the experiment "Building Blocks" (page 55), children make two models, an animal cell and an animal. The cell model contains these parts: the **cell membrane** (the lining around the cell which holds the cell together), the **cytoplasm** (the jellylike fluid that the cell parts float in), the **nucleus** (the control center of the cell which directs all the cell's activities), and the **mitochondria** (the power stations of the cell where food and oxygen react to produce the energy needed for the cell to work and live).

The four parts of the cell model made in "Building Blocks" are common to both animals and plants. Two cell parts found only in plant cells are **chloroplasts** (green bodies in which food for the plant is made) and a **cell wall** (a stiff wall-like structure on the outside of the cell membrane). In the experiment "Stiff" (page 58), a basic model of a plant cell is made to show that it isn't bones that give plants their structure but the stiff cell wall. How water contributes to the firmness of a plant's structure is also shown.

Predators and Prey

A **predator** is an animal that hunts and eats other animals. The animal that becomes the meal for the predator is called the **prey**. Because of **camouflage** (colors and/or patterns on an animal's body that help the animal blend in with its environment), some animals avoid becoming a meal. **Chameleons** are lizards whose skin can change color. The color changes are usually from green to yellow or brown. These changes are a result of changes in temperature, light, and even the lizard's moods. Often the changes make the animal blend in with its environment, but not always. The experiment "Blending" (page 62) demonstrates how colors can protect an animal from its predators.

Many animals, such as cats, are **nocturnal** (active at night). Cats need to be able to see well in order to hunt small animals in the dark, so their eyes have special features. The experiment "Bright Eyes" (page 65) demonstrates two of these features. First, the shiny reflective layer at the back of the eye, called the **tapetum**, reflects light and causes the eye to glow. This increases the chances that the light will come in contact with the light-sensitive cells inside the cat's eye. Second, the **pupil** (the black opening in the center of the eye) **dilates** (enlarges) in the dark to let in more light.

Body Temperature

Some animals, such as dogs, are not able to sweat to cool off, so instead they pant. When a dog pants, water from its tongue **evaporates** (changes from a liquid to a gas). In the process, the water takes heat energy away from the skin, causing the skin to cool. The experiment "Chill Out" (page 69) demonstrates the cooling effect of evaporation.

The fur and feathers of animals **insulate** (reduce the escape of heat) their bodies. Some animals that live in very cold environments also have a thick layer of **blubber** (insulating fat) under their skin. The experiment "Over-coats" (page 71) demonstrates the insulating ability of fur or feathers and blubber.

Animal Movement

Even though some squirrels are called flying squirrels, they cannot fly. These squirrels have special flaps of skin stretched between their front and hind legs. When the squirrel leaps from one branch to another, the skin is stretched out like sails to help it glide. The experiment "Glider" (page 74) demonstrates how flying squirrels glide.

Liquids, such as water, push up on objects in it. This upward force is called **buoyancy**. If the weight of the object is spread out, the water under the object can lift it to the surface and hold it there. Thus, the object floats. A fish rises or sinks by taking in or releasing air from a balloonlike organ called a **swim bladder**. This air changes the weight of the fish, but it is the change in size that affects it most. As the amount of air inside the fish's bladder increases, the fish enlarges. Since it takes up more space in the water, there is more water pushing up on it. Thus, it rises. The experiment "Floaters" (page 77) demonstrates how fish rise and sink in water.

Plant Growth

Germination is the plant process of developing from a seed into a plant. A **seed** is the part of a plant formed in the flower. It contains the **embryo** (the part that develops into a plant) and stored food. Seeds can germinate and grow almost anywhere if they have the right temperature, water, and air. Beans and other seeds from around the kitchen will grow if they have not been cooked or otherwise injured. The heat of cooking will kill the embryo inside the seed. In the experiment "Sprouters" (page 80), children plant beans and other seeds to see whether they will grow.

Growth of a plant toward light is called **phototropism**. *Photo* means light and *tropism* means turning. This type of growth occurs when plant chemicals cause cells on the dark side of the plant stem to grow longer than those on the light side. Longer cell growth on one side of the stem causes the stem to curve.

Thus, the stem curves or turns toward the light. In the experiment "Sun Seekers" (page 83), plants are observed to grow toward sunlight.

Plant Parts

Cacti and other desert plants store water. Some cacti, such as the saguaro, have a pleated surface that allows them to expand with water during wet periods. These cacti may increase in size as much as 20 percent during the rainy season. During times of no rain, they use up their stored water and shrink back to a smaller size and shape. Desert plants have other ways of reducing the amount of water vapor lost through transpiration. Having thick, wavy, coated leaves and stems is one way of doing this. The experiment "Juicy" (page 87) demonstrates how cacti and other desert plants store and retain water.

The flesh of bananas and other fruits, such as pears and apples, discolors when the fruit is peeled and the flesh is exposed to air. This discoloration happens when oxygen in the air combines with the fruit. Vitamin C, which occurs naturally in lemons and other citrus fruits, combines with the oxygen before the oxygen gets to the fruit. The experiment "Browning" (page 90) shows how vitamin C can be used to prevent the darkening of peeled bananas.

Flowers

The oil in many sweet-smelling flowers serves multiple purposes. It is used in making perfume, and it also attracts pollinators, such as insects, to the flowers. Not all flowers have sweet-smelling oils. The rafflesia, a Malaysian plant, smells like rotting meat. The flowers of this plant are pollinated by flies attracted to the stinky smell. In the experiment "Scented" (page 93), children make perfume from the sweet-smelling oil in the petals of garden flowers. They also learn which kinds of insects are attracted to these flowers.

Plants can be temporarily preserved by arranging them between sheets of Contact paper. This method flattens and holds the plant parts as they **dehydrate** (lose water). In the experiment "Keepers" (page 96), children learn this method of preserving plants.

BUGS

Collecting

In the experiment "Trapper" (page 101), children are shown a safe technique for catching insects. Ways of studying insects are also discovered.

A home for crickets is constructed in the experiment "Bug House" (page 104). Children also discover how to tell boy and girl crickets apart.

Changing

The changes insects go through during their life cycle is called **metamorphosis**. The number of changes varies with the insect. Some insects, such as the butterfly, undergo **complete metamorphosis**, which means there are four stages: egg, larva, pupa, and adult. In the metamorphosis of a butterfly, the **larva** (the second stage of complete metamorphosis) is called a **caterpillar**, and the **pupa** (the third, resting stage of complete metamorphosis) is called a **chrysalis**. Some other insects, such as the grasshopper, undergo **incomplete metamorphosis**, which means there are three stages of development: egg, nymph, and adult. A **nymph** is a smaller version of the adult. If the adult has wings, the wings develop during the nymph stage. In the experiment "Around and Around" (page 108), children make models to demonstrate both complete and incomplete metamorphosis.

The firm outside covering of an insect or spider is called an **exoskeleton**. The exoskeleton does not grow as the insect larvae and nymphs grow. Insects in these stages and growing spiders shed their exoskeletons as they grow. This is called **molting**. Generally, adult insects and spiders do not grow. In the experiment "Break Out" (page 111), children experience how a grasshopper nymph breaks out of its exoskeleton and how a butterfly breaks out of its chrysalis.

Moving

All caterpillars are not alike, but they have the same basic body structure, with up to thirteen segments and a head with six simple eyes on each side. They have six "true" legs on the first three body segments. These true legs are generally longer and thinner than the five pairs of shorter, fatter, "false" legs on the middle and four end segments. The true legs become the legs of the adult moth or butterfly that the caterpillar changes into. The ten false legs are used to support and move the growing body of the caterpillar. On the bottom of the false legs, small hooks called **crochets** act as grippers, allowing the caterpillar to hold tightly on to a branch or leaf. The false legs are shed when the caterpillar loses its last skin. In the experiment "Creepers" (page 115), children make a model of the basic body structure of a caterpillar and use it to show how a caterpillar creeps along. Some caterpillars, called loopers or inchworms, have fewer false legs in the middle segment. The false legs on the end inch forward and the middle segment loops upward. The name looper or inchworm comes from this movement.

Fleas are able to jump high because their back legs are long and strong, and have in them a special elastic protein called **resilin**. When a flea bends its legs to begin a jump, the resilin compresses like a spring. When the flea stretches its legs, the resilin springs back to its normal shape. This change catapults the flea upward through the air. In the experiment "Springy" (page 118), children make a paper model of a flea and use various styles of models to stage a flea Olympics.

Communicating

Some bees communicate among themselves by dancing. A female bee that finds a rich supply of nectar returns to the hive and tells the others the location of food supplies by dancing. If the food is close, the bee dances in a circle. If the food is far away, she does the **waggle** dance, which consists of quick movements from side to side down the center line of a figure-eight pattern. The more distant the food, the faster she waggles. In the experiment "Dancers" (page 122), children learn to do the waggle dance and imitate how the rapidity of a bee's waggle tells the other bees how far away the food is.

Fireflies give off light because of chemical changes inside their abdomens. One change turns the light on, and a second change turns it off. The lighted area usually is on the side of the abdomen. The male firefly finds the female by following her flashing lights. Unlike the light from fires and lightbulbs, the light made by fireflies is cool to the touch. The production of light by living things is called **bioluminescence**. In the experiment "Flashers" (page 125), a light stick is used to represent a firefly's light and to make a model of a firefly.

Eating

Insects do not have teeth. A grasshopper is able to chew by grinding its ridged jaws together, whereas a fly eats only liquid through a **proboscis**, a feeding tube that uncoils and is used like a straw. In the experiment "Munchers" (page 129), children discover how grasshoppers and flies eat.

Butterflies eat only nectar and other liquids. They can taste the sweet nectar of flowers with their feet. The taste causes the butterfly to uncoil its proboscis and stick it into the flower to drink. In the experiment "Sippers" (page 132), children use straws to eat like a butterfly and party blowers to see how a proboscis uncoils.

Camouflaging

A **predator** is an animal that hunts and eats other animals. The animal that becomes the meal for the predator is called the **prey**. The colors and/or shape of an animal's body that blend in with its environment are called **camouflage**. In the experiment "Hide-and-Seek" (page 136), children make a model of a walkingstick and other bugs, and use them to demonstrate camouflage.

Many butterflies have wings that are brightly colored on the top side to attract a mate. But generally the reverse side has a dull color with a more confusing pattern that helps to hide the butterfly when it is resting. In the experiment "Top and Bottom" (page 139), children make decorative paper butterfly wings to show how their color helps the butterfly to blend in or stand out.

Spinning

Spiders are bugs that have two body parts and eight legs. A spider's two main body parts are called the **cephalothorax** (combined head and thorax) and the abdomen. Its eight legs are attached to the cephalothorax. A spider generally has eight eyes located on the top and front of its head. The spider releases **silk**, which is a protein that can be pulled from the spider's body by fingerlike parts on the underside of its abdomen called **spinnerets**. In the experiment "Over the Edge" (page 143), children make a model of a spider and learn how a **dragline** (a cord, generally made of two thick strands of silk, by which a spider can suspend itself) protects the spider from falling. When a real spider climbs up its dragline, the dragline disappears as the spider climbs. This is because the spider catches the cord on one of its legs and rolls the silk into a ball as it climbs. The ball is dropped or eaten by the spider.

Unlike insects, spiders undergo very little metamorphosis during their development. The adult generally lays eggs in a silken sac, which may be put in all sorts of places. Some egg sacs are placed in or near the web, and some are carried by the female. The eggs usually hatch in a few weeks. The **spiderlings** (young spiders) usually cut or tear open the egg sac with their jaws and fangs. Spiderlings that hatch during cool fall weather may stay in the sac until warm spring weather arrives. In the experiment "Spiderlings" (page 146), children discover the steps of spider development and find out about the technique that spiderlings use to float through the air and move to new areas. This technique is called **ballooning**.

THE HUMAN BODY

Skin

The protective outer covering on your body is called **skin**. There are two layers of skin, an outer layer called the **epidermis**, and the under layer, called the **dermis**.

Skin doesn't fit tightly around your entire body. Instead, it is loose at **joints** (a place where two bones come together) to allow movement. The experiment "Pleated" (page 151) shows that there is extra skin around joints, such as the elbows and the knuckles in fingers.

The outer layers of skin are flat, dead cells called **squames**. Squames have a hexagonal (six-sided) shape and overlap each other at the edges, like cards that are shuffled. Flat layers of squames plus natural body oil called **sebum** make most of your skin almost waterproof. But the skin on the tips of your fingers and toes is less waterproof. This skin has many more layers of cells than other parts of your body, but it lacks the **glands** (body parts that produce fluids) that make sebum. Because of its thickness and because it is less water resistant, the skin on your fingers and toes soaks up many times as much water as other skin layers when you stay in water a long time. The swollen squames are too big to lie flat, so the skin wrinkles. The experiment "Puckered" (page 153) models the puckering of the skin on toes and fingers, and shows how waterproof most of your skin is.

Hair

Strands of hair trap air between them. The hair and the trapped air are **insulators** (materials that slow down the transfer of energy such as heat). Hair on the body also acts as a collector to prevent foreign materials from entering the body through the nose, ears, and eyes. The experiment "Hairy" (page 157) demonstrates that hair protects the body from losing heat and shows how hair traps airborne particles.

Hair is straight, wavy, or curly because of its shape. A cross section of a strand of straight hair shows that it has the most rounded shape. The flatter the cross section, the curlier the hair strand. High **humidity** (water in air) causes hair to change shape. This is because parts of the hair strand absorb water and get fatter. This makes the hair twist and bend in different directions. Some curly hair gets straighter, and other curly hair gets curlier. Some straight hair may get slightly curly. The experiment "Curly" (page 160) uses models to show why hair curls.

Skeleton

All the bones of your body make up the **skeletal system.** This system provides the framework that allows you to stand upright and protects delicate internal body parts. A baby has more than 300 bones, but some of the bones eventually join together. An adult has about 206 bones.

The central support for your entire body is your **spine** (backbone). It is made up of 26 linked bones, called **vertebrae**, which become progressively larger down your back. Through the back of the vertebrae is a bundle of nerves called the **spinal cord.** You are able to bend because your vertebrae are separated. The disks between the vertebrae keep the bones from grinding together. The experiment "Movable" (page 163) uses a model to show how flexible the backbone is. It also demonstrates that you are taller in the morning. This is because, during the night, the liquid-filled disks and the vertebrae separate. Standing squeezes out liquid in the disks because **gravity** (a force that pulls things toward the center of the earth) pulls the vertebrae together.

The hard part of bones is made up mainly of the chemical **calcium phosphate**. Fibers called **collagen** run through the calcium phosphate. Calcium phosphate gives bones firmness and strength, and collagen gives them flexibility. The experiment "Rubbery" (page 166) shows how to remove calcium from a bone, leaving the rubbery collagen. Eating things with vinegar will not make your bones rubbery. Your body's bones are not soaked in the vinegar. This experiment also shows how the shape of your thigh bone gives it strength. The hollow, cylindrical or can shape of some bones not only increases their strength, but makes them lightweight.

Circulation

When the skin is cut, blood vessels are usually cut. Blood flows out of the cut vessel until small blood cells rush to the wound. (**Cells** are basic body units.) These cells, called **platelets**, help to form the threadlike fibers that make a web at the wound opening. Blood is trapped in the webbing and forms a **clot** (a lump that forms in a liquid). The clot dries and hardens into a crust called a **scab** and the wound is closed. If you pull a scab off, the wound can start bleeding again.

A **bruise** is an injury in which the skin is discolored but not broken. The discoloration is due to blood that leaks out broken blood vessels into **tissue** (groups of similar cells that form various body parts) beneath the skin. The color of the bruise changes because of special blood cells called **phagocytes**. The job of phagocytes is to keep the inside of the body clean by eating such things as invading **germs** (microscopic organisms that can cause diseases) and spilled blood under the skin. The color of a bruise changes as phagocytes eat the blood cells and chemicals destroy their once-red pigments. The experiment "Plugged" (page 170) models the clotting of blood and bruising.

Heart sounds are the sounds made by the heart's **valves** (flaps of tissue that control the flow of blood or other liquids in the body) as they open and shut. The softer "lub" sound is from the valves shutting in the top chambers of the heart. The louder "dub" sound is from the heart valves shutting off the big vessels leaving the heart. The heart pumps blood to carry nutrients and oxygen to all the cells of your body. **Nutrients** are substances in food that are needed for body growth, repair, and energy. **Oxygen** is a gas in the air that is needed for life. The experiment "Lub-Dub" (page 173) uses a homemade **stethoscope** (an instrument used to listen to sounds made by the body, specifically the heart and lungs) to hear a heartbeat.

Respiration

When you breathe in, air moves in through your nose or mouth and down your **trachea** (windpipe) to your **lungs** (organs in your chest that fill with air when you breathe in). The **diaphragm** (a sheet of muscle that forms the floor of the body's chest) controls your breathing. You **inhale** (breathe in) when the diaphragm moves down. You **exhale** (breathe out) when the diaphragm moves up. The experiment "In and Out" (page 176) shows how you breathe.

Your breath forms a small cloud on cold days because it contains water. The cold air makes the water change from a gas to tiny liquid drops. The cloud quickly disappears because the liquid droplets change back into a gas that cannot be seen. In the experiment "Frosty" (page 179), you can see and collect the water in your breath.

Digestion

Before food can be used by the body, it must be chopped into small pieces so that it is easier to **digest** (change into a form that can be used by the body). Your teeth chop up your food. Chewing is the first step in the digestion of food. The experiment "Choppers" (page 183) shows the jobs of different-shaped teeth. Children also build a model of teeth.

The **digestive system** is a group of body parts that break food down into usable nutrients and **waste** (the nonuseful solid part of food that exits the body through the anus; called feces or stool). The **anus** is the opening at the lower end of the large intestine. The experiment "Tube Chute" (page 186) shows the basic parts of the digestive system and their approximate sizes for a child.

Senses

You interact with the world around you through your five basic senses: sight, taste, smell, hearing, and touch. The experiment "Big and Little" (page 190) shows how the **pupil** (black dotlike opening in the colored part of the eye) changes size and thus controls the amount of light entering the eye. White light is made up of the different rainbow colors of light: red, orange, yellow, green, blue, indigo, and violet. These different colors are reflected off objects of the same color. When white light from a camera flash enters the pupil of the eye, the red part of white light reflects off the red blood vessels at the back of the eye. The more dilated the pupil, the more red light reflected off the eyes and the redder the eyes in the photo.

To experience taste, chemicals from food must first dissolve in your mouth's saliva. This liquid then moves into the openings at the top of the **taste buds** (cells on the tongue that identify different tastes) and a taste message is sent to your brain. The experiment "Tasty" (page 193) identifies the four basic tastes. It also shows how smell affects the flavor of foods.

APPENDIX B
Teacher's Guide

Science has a magical appeal for a young child. When parents, guardians, and teachers support and encourage that inborn gift of curiosity, children learn that science is fun! This book is for parents and teachers to share with children ages 4–7. It is designed to help you and your class explore together the fun of science.

The experiments in this book use the discovery-learning technique. In discovery learning, the child learns by observing, organizing, measuring, predicting, describing, and forming conclusions. The best way to achieve this is to allow children to learn by discovering things on their own rather than by "being told all about it." Discovery learning does not mean that the teacher allows children to do whatever they want. It is a guided learning experience with you as the director. You facilitate the learning process by asking leading questions while refraining from giving too many direct answers. The discovery-learning method aids in better memory retention, and completing proven experiments can give children the necessary feeling of success that raises their self-esteem.

Janice VanCleave's Big Book of Play and Find Out Science Projects includes experiments relating to broad topics in science. The more than 50 hands-on experiments, inspired by questions from real kids, are set up in a "cookbook" format—follow the recipe and the results are guaranteed. The materials are all inexpensive and easy to find.

The book also contains an appendix that includes a brief summary of the concepts presented in each chapter. This appendix (Appendix A) is just for you. It will help you to understand the basic science behind each experiment and to answer any questions your students might have.

GUIDELINES FOR USING EXPERIMENTS SUCCESSFULLY IN THE CLASSROOM

Get to Know the Experiment

Read the experiment completely before starting, and practice doing the experiment prior to class time. This increases your understanding of the topic and makes you more familiar with the procedure and the materials. If you know the experiment well, it will be easier for you to give instructions, answer questions, and expound on the topic.

Each experiment answers a question about a child's world. The experiments are formatted as follows:

- **Round Up These Things:** A list of supplies you'll need to do the main project.

- **Later You'll Need:** A list of supplies you'll need if you are going to do the additional activities described in "More Fun Things to Know and Do."

- **Let's Find Out:** Step-by-step instructions on how to perform the main experiment. Steps marked by the symbol "Adult Step" should be done by an adult. Young children may also need assistance with some of the other steps depending on their stage of development.

- **So Now We Know:** A simple explanation of what the main experiment shows.

- **More Fun Things to Know and Do:** Additional facts and experiments.

Collect and Organize Supplies Well Ahead of Time

You will be less frustrated and more successful if you have all the necessary materials for the experiments ready for instant use. If you have storage room, label boxes with the experiment name, and store until needed again. Be sure to replace used items in each box before storing it. You may want to keep labeled boxes filled with basic supplies that are used in many projects, such as scissors, tape, marking pens, and so forth.

Set Up a Discovery Center

While the experiments in this book can be used with large groups, they were designed for small groups with one-on-one adult guidance. An area in the classroom called the Discovery Center can be designated for an independent or a small group science activity. How you set up and use the center is your choice, but here's one suggestion. First have a Circle Time: a whole-group activity directed by the teacher. At Circle Time introduce and demonstrate the main experiment of a chapter with assistance from student helpers. Try reading the procedure for one of the steps and displaying the illustration that goes with it, then demonstrate how to do what you just read. You may wish to stop short of showing the final step so that the students themselves experience seeing the results for the first time. Remember, information is more likely to be retained if the learner is an active, integral part of the learning process. Always emphasize that safety is of the utmost importance and that the instructions should be followed exactly.

After you have gone through the experiment in Circle Time, you could use the Dis-

---

TIPS ON MATERIALS

- Some experiments call for water. If you don't have a sink in your classroom, you can supply water in a plastic soda bottle. Waste liquids can be poured into a gallon milk jug for easy carrying to the nearest sink. A large funnel in the jug makes it easy to pour in the liquids.

- Extra paper towels or sponges are always handy for accidental spills.

- For non-liquid cleanup, have available adult- and child-size brooms and dustpans.

- To save time, you can precut some of the materials (except string, see below), either to the exact size needed or to a slightly larger size if measuring is going to be part of the activity.

- Do not cut string in advance, because it generally gets twisted and is difficult to separate. You and the children can measure and cut the string together.

- The specific sizes and types of containers in the material lists are those used when these projects were tested. This doesn't mean that substituting a different type of container will result in a project failure. Substitution of supplies should be a judgment made after you read a project to determine the use of the supplies. For example, you could replace a 1-quart (1-liter) pitcher with a jar that is equal, or nearly equal, to 1 quart (1 liter).

- For large groups, multiply the supplies by the number in the group so that each person can perform the project individually. Some of the supplies can be shared, so read the procedure to determine this ahead of time.

- Give students cautions and instructions on how to use each tool, such as scissors.

- Students should never put any of the materials in their mouths unless they have been given specific instructions to do so (as when a tasting experiment is being performed).

- During tasting experiments, special care should be taken to provide a sanitary work area. Paper plates or cups and plastic spoons or toothpicks should be used to hold food, and then discarded after each use.

- Supplies or experiment results should not be removed from the classroom unless special permission has been given.

- Keep soap, water, and paper towels handy for washing hands after experiments.

- When using straws, balloons, or other materials that are placed in the mouth, be sure each student has his or her own and they do not share. Dispose of all such materials as soon as each experiment is finished.

- Have all supplies ready so that the project starts quickly. Busy children are more attentive and less likely to be off task. When possible, allow students to be your helpers in setting out and putting away supplies.

- Limit the science activity time. If the project has several parts, do some of them at a later time. Children are more attentive during short, quick, fun activities. The experiments in this book are designed to be brief to match the typical attention span of young children.

TRY THIS TECHNIQUE/STICKERS EXPERIMENT

In the following example, the scientific objective is for students to discover that magnets are attractive to metals, but not to paper.

Suggestions for Teaching "Stickers"

Follow these steps to teach this experiment in the classroom.

1 Perform the instruction yourself before introducing it to the class. Prepare all needed materials.

2 Introduce the experiment during the Circle Time. Hold the book so that the group can see the illustration as you read the "I wonder" question being asked by the child in the illustration.

3 Encourage the class to give answers to the "I wonder" question, then say "Let's find out!"

4 Read the procedure for the experiment and demonstrate each step to the group. For very young children, you may decide to modify the procedure steps. Instead of the child drawing a rectangle, a paper with a rectangle printed on it may be used.

5 Prepare the class to perform the experiment. It is at this point that you have the option to direct the class as a whole in performing the experiment or to work in the Discovery Center with smaller groups of children.

covery Center for independent or small group study. Provide supplies and instructions so that students can duplicate and learn more about the experiment presented during Circle Time. Many of the "More Fun Things to Know and Do" sections provide activities for this center.

Keeping Students On Task

Very young children, and many older ones, find it difficult to be attentive for long periods of time. Hands-on, individual, or small group instruction certainly helps. While there is no magic solution to the problem, the following can help make children more attentive:

6 For very young children or children requiring extra assistance, read the procedure aloud again as the children perform the experiment themselves. After each step, observe the progress of each student to make sure he or she is ready for the next step. Proceed until all the steps have been read.

7 Allow all the children to experiment with their covered magnets for a few minutes. Then, have another Circle Time. Ask the group the following questions and allow time for individual answers:

- Does paper stick to magnets? *(no)*
- Do paper clips stick to magnets? *(yes)*
- What are paper clips made of? *(metal)*
- Do magnets stick to refrigerators? *(yes)*
- What are refrigerators made of? *(metal)*

8 Use the "So Now We Know" section and information in Appendix A to explain why magnets stick to some metals.

Suggestions for Teaching "More Fun Things to Know and Do"

Use the additional thematically-related experiment in this section to discover other fun things that can be done with a magnet and paper.

1 Prepare and demonstrate using a magnet to move paper figures on top of a shoe box.

2 Generic paper figures can be predrawn and copies made. Depending on the time available for the experiment and the capabilities of the children, you may wish to precut the generic figures. Another method would be to cut pictures from magazines and glue them on heavier paper.

CURRICULUM CONNECTIONS

Literature

In addition to the reading skills developed through reading the experiments, there are many opportunities to connect science and

---

TIPS ON GETTING PARENTS INVOLVED

- While all the supplies needed for the experiments are inexpensive and readily available, it can't hurt to get some help in obtaining them. Here's one area where parents can get involved. With administrative permission, you may wish to send home a list of general supplies that will be needed during the school year or just supplies needed for a specific experiment. Be sure to make the request optional and not to ask for too many supplies, or parents might think you are asking too much of them.

- You may also wish to involve parents in the science activities themselves. Invite parents to sign up for a specific date to help with a science experiment in class.

Give parents a copy of the experiment ahead of time so they can review and possibly try out the experiment on their own. Then, in class time each parent could supervise the Discovery Center.

- You could assign each student a homework project of explaining to their family what they learned from doing an experiment in the class. They may even want to direct their family in performing the experiment at home. It is especially helpful if you send home a science box with instructions and materials if possible. Include a note containing a list of materials that could be replaced before the kit is returned to school.

reading skills. Students can be encouraged to read more about the topic of their science experiment in books and magazines. Have books available for this extension of the science experiment. Reading and science can be taught by selecting conceptually and factually correct works of fictional children's literature. For example, *The Carrot Seed*, by Ruth Krauss (New York: HarperCollins), could be used to teach about seeds when performing the experiment "Sprouters."

Art

Many of the activities in this book encourage artistic skills as well as scientific investigation. For "Stickers," students add their own features to the stand-up figures and could design different figures, such as those of animals. Artistic skills can be expressed in designing results diagrams and project displays as well as in making scientific models. You could also use science information as subjects for skits, puppet shows, poems, or songs that children create or help to create. For example, a few props, such as a zippered sleeping bag and scarfs for gossamer wings, can be used to act out the metamorphosis of a butterfly.

Math

In addition to basic arithmetic skills, many of the experiments require measuring skills to find accurate length, volume, or weight. After an experiment, you may choose to evaluate the math skills acquired by each student by asking the students individually to repeat a procedure, such as measuring the length of a string or counting out a specific number of beans.

Geography

Science can be related to specific places. For example, when you are studying about plants and animals, use a map to point out where specific animals or plants are found. Be sure to have maps and globes on hand when you are going to have students do an experiment with a geographical connection.

History

Science is not just new discoveries. It is also a historical discipline. Take time to talk about historic events and people related to science, such as the first man who walked on the moon. An ongoing simple timeline to which you can add labels indicating what, when, and where can be hung across an area of the room. Nonfiction stories about scientists can be used to introduce scientific events and what was happening in the world when these events occurred.

Glossary

air A mixture of gases, mainly nitrogen and oxygen.

anus The opening at the lower end of the large intestine.

atmosphere The layer of air surrounding the earth.

atoms Tiny particles from which all things are made.

ballooning A technique that spiderlings use to float through the air and move to new areas.

battery A device that uses chemicals to produce an electric current.

bioluminescence The production of light by living things.

blubber A thick layer of insulating fat under the skin of some animals that live in cold environments, such as seals, whales, and walruses.

bruise An injury in which the skin is discolored but not broken. Discoloration is due to blood released from broken blood vessels into tissue.

buoyancy The upward force that a liquid, such as water, exerts on objects floating in it.

calcium phosphate A chemical in bones that gives them firmness and strength.

camouflage Colors and/or patterns that conceal an object by matching the background.

canopy The part of a parachute that captures the air.

caterpillar Butterfly or moth larva.

cell membrane The lining around a cell that holds the cell together.

cell wall The stiff wall-like structure on the outside of the cell membrane of plants.

cell The basic unit of all living things.

cephalothorax The combined head and thorax of a spider.

chameleon A lizard with skin that can change from green to yellow or brown.

chemical change A change, such as oxidation, in which materials change into something else.

chloroplasts Green bodies in a plant cell that contain chlorophyll and in which food for the plant is made.

chrysalis Butterfly pupa.

clot A lump that forms in a liquid.

collagen Fibers of protein such as in bones that give them their flexibility.

compass An instrument used to determine direction by means of a free-swinging magnetic needle that points to the earth's magnetic north pole.

complete metamorphosis Four-staged metamorphosis: egg, larva, pupa, and adult.

crochets Small hooks on the bottom of a caterpillar's false legs that act as grippers, allowing the caterpillar to hold tightly onto a branch or leaf.

current electricity A form of energy associated with the movement of electric charges.

cytoplasm The jellylike fluid that the parts of a cell float in.

dehydrate To lose water or to remove water from.

density   A comparison of weight and size.

dermis   The under layer of skin.

diaphragm   A sheet of muscle that forms the floor of the body's chest.

digest   To change food into a form that can be used by the body.

digestive system   The group of body parts that break food down into nutrients.

dilate   To enlarge.

dragline   A cord, generally made of two thick strands of silk, by which a spider can suspend itself.

elasticity   The ability of a material to return to its original shape after being pushed or pulled out of shape.

electric circuit   The path that electricity follows.

electrons   Negative electric charges in an atom.

epidermis   The outer layer of skin.

evaporate   To change from a liquid to a gas due to absorption of energy, such as heat.

exhale   To breathe out.

exoskeleton   The outside covering of the body of an insect or a spider.

expand   To spread out.

flexible   Having elasticity.

force   A push or pull in a given direction.

germination   The plant process of developing from a seed into a plant.

germs   Microscopic organisms that can cause diseases.

gland   A body part that produces a fluid.

gravity   The force that pulls everything toward the center of the earth.

humidity   Water in air.

incomplete metamorphosis   Three-staged metamorphosis: egg, nymph, and adult.

inertia   The resistance to change in motion.

inhale   To breathe in.

insulate   To reduce the escape of energy, such as heat, from an object.

insulator   A material that slows down the transfer of energy, such as heat.

joint   The point where bones come together.

larva (plural **larvae**)   The young wormlike form of an insect during the second stage of complete metamorphosis.

lungs   Organs in your chest that fill with air when you breathe in.

magnetic field   The area around a magnet in which its magnetic forces can be detected.

magnetic north pole   The area near the northernmost point on the earth toward which the north poles of all magnets are attracted.

matter   Anything that takes up space and has weight.

metamorphosis   Changes in the life cycle of an insect. See also **complete metamorphosis** and **incomplete metamorphosis**.

mitochondria (singular **mitochondrion**)   The power stations of a cell where food and oxygen react to produce the energy needed for the cell to work and live.

molt   To shed an exoskeleton.

nocturnal   Active at night.

north pole of a magnet   The end of a magnet that points to the earth's magnetic north pole.

nucleus   The control center of a cell that directs all the cell's activities.

nutrients   Substances in food that are needed for growth, repair, and energy.

nymph   The second stage of incomplete metamorphosis. The nymph is smaller than the adult insect and has no functional wings.

oxygen   A gas in the air needed for life.

phagocytes   Special blood cells that eat germs and other things, such as spilled blood under the skin, to keep the inside of the body clean.

phototropism   The growth of a plant toward light.

pitch   The high or low quality of a sound.

platelets   Blood cells that form fibers used to clot blood where blood vessels are cut.

predator   An animal that hunts and eats other animals.

prey   An animal that becomes a meal for a predator.

proboscis   The feeding tube of certain insects, such as flies and butterflies.

protons   Positive electric charges in an atom.

pupa (plural **pupae**)   The third stage of complete metamorphosis between the larval and the adult.

pupil   The black opening in the center of the eye.

rainbow   An arc-shaped band of colors in the sky.

resilin   Elastic protein.

scab   A crust over a wound formed by the drying and hardening of blood clots.

sebum   Natural body oil.

seed   A plant part formed in the flower and containing the embryo and stored food.

shadow   The dark area cast upon a surface by an object that blocks light.

silk   A protein produced by bugs, such as caterpillars and spiders, that can be pulled from the bug's body into smooth, fine, or thick strands.

skeletal system   The body's framework, made up of all the bones of the body.

skin   The protective outer covering on the body.

spider   A bug that has two body parts and four pairs of legs, and that is capable of producing silk from spinnerets.

spiderlings   Young spiders.

spinal cord   Bundle of nerves running from the brain through the vertebrae of the spine.

spine   Backbone.

spinnerets   The fingerlike body parts located at the end and on the underside of a spider's abdomen, where spiders and certain larvae release silk from their bodies.

squames   Flat, dead cells in the outer skin layers.

static electricity   The buildup of stationary electric charges in one place.

stethoscope   An instrument used to listen to the heart and lungs.

swim bladder   A balloonlike organ that helps a fish rise or sink by taking air in or releasing it from the organ.

tapetum   The shiny reflective layer at the back of the eye of some animals, such as cats.

taste buds   Cells on the tongue that identify different tastes.

tissue   Groups of similar cells that form various body parts.

trachea   Windpipe.

valve   A flap of tissue that controls the flow of blood or other liquids in the body.

vertebrae   Separate bones in the spine.

waggle   Quick movements from side to side.

waste   The nonuseful solid parts of food that exit the body through the anus.

weight   A force caused by gravity.